THE POETICS OF WRONGNESS

RACHEL ZUCKER

THE POETICS
OF WRONGNESS

WAVE BOOKS

SEATTLE AND NEW YORK

Published by Wave Books

www.wavepoetry.com

Copyright © 2023 by Rachel Zucker

Wave Books titles are distributed to the trade by

Consortium Book Sales and Distribution

Phone: 800-283-3572 / SAN 631-760X

Library of Congress Cataloging-in-Publication Data

Names: Zucker, Rachel, author.

Title: The poetics of wrongness / Rachel Zucker.

Description: First edition. | Seattle : Wave Books, [2023]

Series: Bagley Wright Lecture Series | Includes bibliographical references.

Identifiers: LCCN 2022045156 | ISBN 9781950268702 (paperback)

Subjects: LCSH: Poetics. | LCGFT: Lectures. | Essays.

Classification: LCC PS3626.U26 P64 2023 | DDC 814/.6—dc23/eng/20220923

LC record available at https://lccn.loc.gov/2022045156

Designed by Crisis

Printed in the United States of America

9 8 7 6 5 4 3 2 1

First Edition

For my Students

>*who are always*
>*also my teachers*
>*especially (but not only)*
>*Isaac Ginsberg Miller*

For my Teachers

>*especially (but not only)*
>*my first teachers*
>*Diane Wolkstein &*
>*Benjamin Zucker*

For You

>*—audience/*
>*reader/listener/*
>*conversationalist/*
>*beloved-other*

& For Now

>*impossible continuous*
>*all-there-is*

THE POETICS OF WRONGNESS, AN UNAPOLOGIA

1

WHAT WE TALK ABOUT WHEN WE
TALK ABOUT THE CONFESSIONAL AND
WHAT WE SHOULD BE TALKING ABOUT

39

A VERY LARGE CHARGE: THE ETHICS
OF "SAY EVERYTHING" POETRY

82

WHY SHE COULD NOT WRITE A LECTURE
ON THE POETICS OF MOTHERHOOD

113

AUTHOR'S NOTE

157

APPENDIX: SELECTED PROSE (2010–2020)

167

SELECTED BIBLIOGRAPHY AND WORKS CITED

210

ACKNOWLEDGMENTS

215

THE POETICS OF WRONGNESS

THE POETICS
OF WRONGNESS,
AN UNAPOLOGIA

I'm writing this lecture in the middle of a particular night in my particular life. This is relevant. Three years ago I was asked to write these lectures, and it seemed impossible. I'd never given lectures. I imagined that giving a lecture required me to tell other people what I think or what I know, which is not really my style. Or, perhaps giving lectures would require me to tell people what *they* should think, which is *really* not my style. What is my style, you wonder? I'm getting to that.

Stay with me, stay in the present, this moment, for a moment. I am, at this particular time in my particular life, the mother of three sons now aged sixteen, fourteen, and eight. This is relevant.

What you need to know about this experience is that I am always wrong. My body is wrong; my presence is wrong. The only thing more wrong is my absence. When I am present, it is embarrassing. When I am absent, it is wounding.

I have learned from my fourteen-year-old that I am always "not listening," even when I think I am listening. I am "not helping," even when I am trying to help. I "don't get it," even when I am trying to understand. "Weren't you ever embarrassed by *your* parents?" he asks when he doesn't want me to meet him after the movie he is going to with his friends. Yes, I say. I was embarrassed by my mother every moment of every day and night when I was your age, I do not say. But it is (unpleasant) news to me that I am now *that* mother, that embarrassing mother, although the fact that this is news is probably proof that I wasn't listening, that I don't get it, that everything about me is wrong.

My sixteen-year-old doesn't find me personally embarrassing or flawed. From him I discover that I am, rather, universally flawed, mistaken, existentially unredeemable. My wrongness is part of the human condition; I am just one not very interesting specimen of general disappointment. With surprising patience, a raised eyebrow, and frequent deep sighing, he explains the many ways in which my ideas about gender, race, mathematics, science, economics, politics, history, psychology, and countless other topics are outdated, erroneous, and sometimes reprehensible.

My just-turned-eight-year-old vaulted from his toddler phase, in which everything anyone said or did was indisputably wrong if it conflicted with what he wanted, directly into his Woody Allen phase, in which he daily confronts me with questions like: "Can you tell me *one thing* that matters after the world ends? Nothing? See? So nothing matters, right?" or, "If everyone dies, then why does being a good person while you're alive matter because eventually you're going to die and everyone you ever help will also die?" There are no right answers to these questions, and this makes me both wrong and profoundly disappointing. Also, I am specifically wrong about everything having to do with soccer, football, music, the appropriate volume of music, the purpose of school (that there is a purpose), whether so-and-so is a nice person or not, what is funny and what is not funny, what is too rough or dangerous, and the matter of playing ball in the apartment. In other words: everything important.

Well, you might be thinking, "Being a parent is like that." But it's not just my kids.

This is the summer—eighteen years into my marriage—that everything I say hurts my husband and everything he says hurts me. We misunderstand each other. Our words come out wrong or are taken wrong. Our tone is wrong even if the words don't wound. If we stop talking, we descend into a terrifying hopelessness.

Stay with me; this is relevant.

Two days ago it was gently revealed to me that the three lectures I'd spent seven months researching and writing are too long, about too many things, simultaneously unfounded and overly informational, too personal and too impersonal—basically: failures. Perhaps (with work) these drafts could become essays, but they are not lectures, said my editor.

So, to summarize: my math is wrong, my logic is wrong, my presence is wrong, my absence is wrong. My gender is wrong insofar as I come from a mode of thinking in which I believe that gender is a fixed trait rather than a fluid, social construct, infinitely complicated and slippery. Being male would make me more wrong but being female is also wrong, and conflating gender with race or sexual preference is wrong. My heterosexuality and whiteness make me wrong, always and all the time, in the sense that they confer unto me privileges at great cost to others so that any "rightness" I have in the sense of power or agency is wrongly mine and part of what makes me wrong in the world and certainly part of what makes the world so very, very wrong.

At forty-three, I am too young and too old. Old people look at me wistfully, teenagers with disgust, children with distrust. Everything about me makes someone extremely angry—who does she think she is? Who do I think I am? And what does this have to do with poetry?

In this climate of wrongness it is difficult to say anything. This isn't new, it is just more apparent to me than ever before. The volume of my wrongness is turned up so high it's impossible to ignore and difficult to shout over. To say anything (even to say "I'm wrong") is wrong—white people should listen. But, simultaneously, to be silent, meek, and/or apologetic is wrong—women should be strong and assertive. And speaking of "this climate": I am one of everyone who is irreparably destroying the Earth. I am more wrong than my children can even imagine. And what woke me up in the middle of this night was the realization that all this wrongness is both excruciating and exactly what I need to talk about.

Over the course of the past seven months, writing about photography, confessional poetry, and the ethical considerations of writing about real people, I was trying to build a case for my thinking and convince you that my ideas were right. I wanted you to feel that my ideas were interesting and worth your time. In this way, I'd abandoned what made me a poet and the very nature of my poetics.

I first started writing poetry (and still write it) because the world, its people, and their ideas are wrong, insane, immoral, flawed, or unimaginably terrible. I write because I feel wrong, sad, crazy, disappointed, disappointing, and unimaginably terrible. I write to expose wrongness and to confess wrongness, yet I sense that doing so is futile at best and more likely compounds wrongness.

I write *against*. My poetics is a poetics of opposition and provocation that I never outgrew. Against the status quo or the powers that be, writing out of and into wrongness.

Here's my current definition of a poet: "I am wrong and you are wrong and I'm willing to say it, therefore I am a poet."

A poet is one who feels wrong in a wrong world and is willing to speak even when doing so proves her wrong, ugly, broken, and complicit. This is not the same as saying that I write poetry to "feel better" or to be forgiven or that the goal of poetry is to "right wrongs." Perhaps some people feel better when they write poetry. Perhaps some poems make the world less wrong. What I'm trying to explain is that a poet's athleticism lies in her ability to stay in and with wrongness. Of being willing to be disliked for being too smart or too stupid, too direct or incomprehensible, elitist or the lowest of the low, and for what? For the privilege of pointing out that everything in the world is wrong (including me).

Wrongness is intrinsic to poetry, which asserts with its most defining formal device—the line break—that the margins of prose are wrong, or—with its attention to diction—that the ways in which we've come to understand and use words are wrong.

Maybe you think I'm wrong in the way I'm using the word "wrong"? Fine. I embrace it. I've never written to please you, even if I liked it when you were pleased.

I write to talk back (sometimes to myself), not to tell you what I think but to figure out what I think, which is always a process of proving myself and others wrong.

It is the job of poems to undermine, to refute, retort, re-see, disrupt. To tell you nicely or aggressively that you are wrong, that the world is fucked up, that all our modes of understanding and expressing are suspect, that there is nothing and no one above reproach or scrutiny.

Poets speak even when it is excruciating, even when no one is listening, often when the poet believes—despite Audre Lorde's admonition, "your silence will not protect you"—that she would be better off staying silent. That's what a poem is: a breaking of silence, a form that makes and then breaks silence over and over. Poetry is the language of pain and grief and hurt and love, and most people in our country hate it but often need it and sometimes find solace or pleasure in it.

I've learned from being a daughter and a mother that finding your parent wrong or being told how wrong you are is a complicated act of attachment, separation, individuation, and love. A parasitic sort of love perhaps, but love—a way of paying attention, of giving a shit. The alternative to being wrong is being ignored.

So, here are a few assertions about poetry. I offer these assertions or (anti-)tenets as an imperfect, (anti-)authority/mouthpiece for the poetics of wrongness. I offer these protestations in the mode of opposition and without apology even though I'm pretty sure that You, audience/reader, along with my sons, my friends, my students, the past, the future, strangers and intimates, both living and dead, are sure to consider what follows to be wrong. As it should be!

I hope You might recognize yourself in these allegations and attestations of wrongness, that You might recognize wrongness in places and forms and people I haven't yet imagined. I hope You will enlarge, emend, revise, subvert, and complexify these sketchy assertions not toward correctness, concision, universality, clarity, timelessness, objectivity, transcendence, or any form of oppressive "rightness," but toward love, liberation, justice, and connection.

I. POETRY SHOULD BE BEAUTIFUL.

John Keats is wrong. Or, "Ode on a Grecian Urn" is wrong when it asserts: "'Beauty is truth, truth beauty,'—that is all / Ye know on earth, and all ye need to know." No.

First of all, the poetics of wrongness has a problem with beauty. To the extent that I even understand what beauty is, I distrust it and reject it as a quality poetry *must* or even *should* pursue or attempt to embody. The poetics of wrongness rejects the notion that poetry is distinguished from other forms of language by its beauty or that the pursuit of beauty is a mandatory occupation of poetry. Beauty is a manipulation of a thing, a bettering, an idealization of the ordinary. Beauty is *not* truth but closer to anti-truth. I can't encounter the word "beauty" without thinking of the "beauty industry," a $425 billion a year industry bent on making me buy things I don't need (and that are bad for me and the environment) in order to look different than how I would otherwise look, with the promise that altering my appearance will make me feel less terrible about myself.

My definition of beauty may be ahistorical; my "beauty" might not be Keats's "beauty," just as I'm sure my idea of truth is not quite the same as his. Perhaps Keats or Keats's urn was referring to a beauty akin to the Platonic notion of "perfection," a just-right proportion that waits to be identified rather than created, a world wherein something is beautiful because it is symmetrical or closely approximates the golden ratio. It is this kind of thinking that underlies Samuel Coleridge's famous delineation of prose and poetry: "I wish our clever young poets would remember my homely definitions of prose and poetry; that is, prose = words in their best order; poetry = the best words in the best order."

Best, perfect, beautiful. I have just as much trouble with perfection or "bestness" as I do with beauty. Perfection and beauty imply flawlessness, and flawlessness is an untruth.

When I was a graduate student at the University of Iowa, the poet Mark Strand came to deliver a lecture. I remember Strand showing paintings of the crucifixion of Jesus as part of a lecture on the old painting masters. I remember him saying that all art is beautiful. I raised my hand—a bold move for a twenty-two-year-old woman in her first year of a graduate program she felt wholly unprepared for and unworthy of—and asked, "What if I want to make art that isn't beautiful?" Strand explained that one could make art about ugly, difficult content, but that for art to succeed it had to transcend ugliness and become beautiful.

Oh, teacher, I say you are wrong. What about Marvin Bell's great love poem "To Dorothy" that begins, "You are not beautiful, exactly. / You are beautiful, inexactly." What about the value of describing, recording, sharing, communicating (as so many great poets do) that which is "inexact" or imperfect or, even: ugly, painful, broken? I too love the well-made thing, but the poetics of wrongness rejects the notion that poetry is a pursuit by which we take the ordinary and put makeup on it, make it better, make it "best." The notion that art *must be* the rendering of the ordinary into the transcendent or extraordinary is not only wrong but is ultimately part of a system of thinking that has been used to oppress, enslave, torment, and destroy.

The poetics of wrongness rejects flawlessness. The poetics of wrongness is only interested in perfection as a manifestation of the Greek notion of *teleios*, or "completeness," because completeness or perfection includes the flaws, the weeds, and the poet's desire to write, which is a necessary and necessarily flawed endeavor. But even if we replace

Keats's or Strand's "beauty" with a notion of perfection or completeness that includes flaws and wrongness, I still have a problem with the equation of beauty and truth. The relationship between *teleios* and truth is not a simple, synonymous "is"! The relationship between beauty and truth is wildly complicated, complex, and impossible to define.

Writing as I am, in the middle of this night, at the beginning of the twenty-first century, it is impossible to consider the word "beauty" without thinking of the myriad unconscionable atrocities that have been committed in the name of "beauty" or beauty's metonyms: perfection, purity, normalcy, goodness, godliness.

Even before the Nazi masterminds (many of them failed artists) turned an obsession with white supremacist aesthetics into genocidal action, beauty had been used as a weapon, a weapon particularly used to define and control women, racialized and colonized peoples, outsiders, the poor, the elderly, the infirm, or differently abled.

Beauty, patriarchy, race, and other binary systems of worth and worthlessness almost always rely on a master/slave construction in order to maintain power. Fascist and capitalist systems both (differently) employ beauty as a gatekeeping strategy and as a passive or explicit way to reify whiteness, ableism, masculinity, straightness, and narrowly (often hypocritically) defined "moral" behaviors. The appreciation and pursuit of beauty is still used today to justify the denial of rights, opportunities, protections, and resources to those who do not embody beauty as defined by those in power.

The poetics of wrongness espouses the pursuit of truth &vs. beauty, which includes an awareness that the pursuit of beauty is inherently flawed, doomed to failure, and inextricably bound up with the history of human cruelty. In the preface to her book *Tender*, Toi Derricotte writes, "The job of the artist is not to resolve or beautify, but to hold complexities, to see and make clear." Whenever the pursuit of beauty leads to equivalency, simplification, or imagined resolution, I reject it. I reject the pursuit of beauty, but welcome the interrogation of beauty as subject matter and also the subversion of "beautiful" forms as one of the ways in which we must "hold complexities" and strive to "see and make clear."

The poetics of wrongness admires poems that enlarge and/or subvert the definition of beauty or attempt to redeem beauty by redefining it—poems about people and bodies and things that have traditionally fallen outside of the frame the beauty-makers or beauty-proclaimers make, such as "poem in praise of menstruation" by Lucille Clifton or almost all of the poems in Sharon Olds's book *Odes*. ("Ode to Menstrual Blood," "Ode to Tampon," "Ode of Withered Cleavage," "Unmatching Legs Ode," "Ode to the Word *Vulva*," "Ode to My Fat," to name a few.) Consider Olds's "Ode to Wattles," which includes the lines:

> I love to be a little
> disgusting, to go as far as I can
> into the thrilling unloveliness
> of an elderwoman's aging . . .

and ends with:

> I bow my head to time,
> and count my withered chins, three five seven
> nine, my muses, my truth which is not
> beauty—my crone beauty, in its first youth.

Take that, Keats! Olds is saying her wattles are "truth" in the sense that they are an unavoidable physical characteristic she possesses as she nears seventy-five and that this truth (of the aging body) is *not* beauty—at least not beauty as defined by a predominantly ageist, misogynist culture. And yet here Olds turns the tables and makes her wattles poem-worthy. She writes an ode to her wattles, writes an entire book of odes to parts of the cis female body, psyche, and experience that traditionally fall outside what "the male mind" has deemed beautiful or poem-worthy. Olds cleverly reworks Keats's last line. The wattles *are* beautiful if we redefine beauty as "crone beauty." Even the phrase "crone beauty" is subversive in that it disrupts the patriarchal, cis-centric view that equates female beauty with youth and potential fertility and therefore imagines the crone as a barren, thin, ugly, sinister archetype. From a matrifocal[1] perspective, a crone is a wise woman, a woman who, because she is beyond her childbearing years, can fully inhabit her own power, freedom, and creative energy. Olds's crone beauty begins, *can only begin*, when her societally defined, wattle-free youth-beauty ebbs away.

Another complex and brilliant response to Keats's "Ode on a Grecian Urn" is the poem "The Facts of Art" by Natalie Diaz. Diaz was born in the late 1970s, raised on the Fort Mojave Indian Reservation, and is a member of the Gila River tribe. In "The Facts of Art," the speaker encounters a Hopi basket from Arizona in a museum in Portsmouth, Virginia. The basket, like the Grecian urn, is an object that tells its own story. In Keats's poem, the urn is a historian who visually depicts "a flow'ry tale more sweetly than our rhyme." In "The Facts of Art," the Hopi basket does not speak sweetly but is a tale-telling relic or artifact of the Hopi people and their art. It also, crucially, serves as inspiration

---

1. Olds's odes are specific to her experiences of cis womanhood. Not all women menstruate or have "childbearing years." Trans and gender-non-binary writers and critics have problematized patriarchal notions of beauty and menopause in non-cis-centric ways.

for the poet to tell the story of white laborers and managers enlisting Hopi men to build a highway across Arizona by cutting into First Mesa. The work does not go easily—blades are burnt out, new blades need to be flown in—and the elders know the BIA (Bureau of Indian Affairs) roads and this highway work are "bad medicine" even before construction disturbs a burial ground, unearthing "the small gray bowls of babies' skulls." When the burial ground is disturbed, the Hopi men refuse to continue working on the road. The white men try to order, beg, and bribe the Hopi workers, but the Hopi men refuse. The white men send their wives up the mesa "to buy baskets from Hopi wives and grandmothers / as a sign of treaty."

Diaz writes:

> When that didn't work, the state workers called the Indians lazy,
>> sent their sunhat-wearing wives back up to buy more baskets—
>> katsinas too—then called the Hopis *good-for-nothings*,
>> before begging them back once more.

This begging and name-calling does not convince the Hopi workers to return, and while the "small bones half-buried in the crevices of mesa— / in the once-holy darkness of silent earth and always-night— / smiled or sighed beneath the moonlight," the white women write letters home praising "their husbands' patience," describing "the lazy savages," the "squalor in their stone and plaster homes," "devilish ceremonies," "barbaric" burial rituals, and (the last line of the poem) "oh, and those beautiful, beautiful baskets."

In this way, the "The Facts of Art" is a well-made poem that at the same time resists beauty both in its making and worldview. The reader learns to be suspicious of everything the whites say and everything said in the language of colonization. Language and naming are tools of violence in the mouths and minds and "letters" of the whites. The white women go to buy baskets from the Hopi wives and grandmothers not as an actual treaty but as a "sign of treaty." The white women fail to notice or note anything of value other than the baskets. By the time the reader reaches the last line—"oh, and those beautiful, beautiful baskets"—the word "beautiful" as uttered and written by these white women is condescending, belittling, malevolent, usurious, and dehumanizing. What (or who?) makes something beautiful? What makes something art? What is the relationship between beauty and art? What are the facts of art? Is the basket "art" because it is preserved in a museum? The basket, once an object of beauty and usefulness, was purchased not for its beauty or utility in the context of its community of origin but in order to bribe (under the guise of "treaty") Hopi workers into desecrating the land. The basket is not only art; it is also a fact of art, an artifact. The basket is an inanimate witness to the systematic oppression and displacement of the Hopi people and the destruction of Hopi art, culture, and lands. This poem is no ode. It is a narrative poem full of quietly spoken outrage. As the poem headbutts Keats[2], it also acknowledges, responds to, and resists received Western forms, including the form it might be closest to: elegy. The poem artfully resists high lyricism, resists being too beautiful,

2. In a *Divedapper* interview with Kaveh Akbar, Diaz talks about her relationship with the canon, saying, "But really the canon for me sometimes feels a little bit strange because where I come from, here on the reservation, in our community, you respect your elders and you know that all the things coming out of you have come through them to you. I'm grabbing onto them, and the energy is moving through me—these words came from somewhere else, somebody else, some other time. But it seems to me when people talk about the canon, that what they are often trying to talk about is assimilation. I really want to headbutt it; you know, we headbutt out here."

resists elegy as a received form that is part of the language and language-making of the conquering whites. In doing so, the poem asks: Who gets to name things? Who gets to make the forms? And, is elegy—typically the form used when lamenting the dead—capable of witnessing and lamenting the loss of entire peoples, languages, and cultures?

Diaz's "The Facts of Art" illuminates the frame of its own making and calls into question the process by which craft becomes art becomes artifact and the way art seldom includes the truth of its own story of production, commodification, and valuation. The basket of Diaz's poem is preserved behind glass in Portsmouth, Virginia. The inclusion of a museum label (also called a "tombstone")—*"woven plaque basket with sunflower design, Hopi, Arizona, before 1935 from an American Indian basketry exhibit in Portsmouth, Virginia"*—insists we think about what is barely outside the "frame" of the poem or the display case in the museum, including the geographical displacement of the basket (and the people who made it), the history of enslaved Africans in Virginia, and in the United States, and the way museums tell "the facts of art" and what museums leave out or misconstrue. The museum becomes a kind of morgue, and "the facts of art" are not just where an art object was made/found, as well as the artist and time period, but the material conditions under which beauty is produced and who or what perished in the making.

The facts of art include the fact that so much (most? all?) art is constructed through violence once you enlarge the frame broadly enough to include the means of art's production.[3] Diaz brings our attention to the

3. See the brilliant poem "study the masters" by Lucille Clifton for a poem that inverts the subject/object and master/mastered positions in order to make visible the positionality of the maker and unseen makers. In doing so, Clifton enlarges the frame to reveal how black female labor has enabled the solitary white male "genius."

violence of making that is erased or disavowed by classical conceptions of art that privilege beauty, transcendence, universality, and an avoidance of biography.

Diaz's poem raises essential questions about art, art-making, beauty, beauty-making, naming, and the commodification of art, beauty, human labor, and land. Is the poet a maker of beauty? Is the job of the poet to make something beautiful or to tell a tale or to bear witness as a historian? What does an artist do when she wants to make something beautiful and moving and brutal and true and at the same time wants to witness and resist the barbarism committed in the name of beauty and civilization?

"What is it like to be so beautiful?" Kenny Fries asks in the beginning of his three-page poem "Beauty and Variations." The question is addressed to a lover by the speaker of the poem who says of himself:

> Beauty, at birth applied, does not transfer
> to my hands. But every night, your hands
>
> touch my scars, raise my twisted limbs to
> graze against your lips. Lips that never
>
> form the words—*you are beautiful*—transform
> my deformed bones into—*what?*—if not beauty.

Fries's scars and twisted limbs are never called beautiful by the lover or by the culture at large, and, yet, what word do we give for the way the act and feeling of physical and emotional love render Fries's body cherished, appreciated, sought after? If beauty is something that is pleasing to the senses, something we want to go toward, something we want more of, why isn't Fries's body beautiful?

"Can only one of us be beautiful? . . . Can blood be beautiful? . . . With no / flaws on your skin—how can I find your heart? . . . How much beauty can a person bear? . . . Was this / birth's plan—to tie desire to my pain, to stain // love's touch with blood?" The questions and intensity of "Beauty and Variations" build until the last section, when Fries asks: "What is beautiful? Who decides?"

The poetics of wrongness is an anti-bourgeois aesthetic of hybridity, alterity, and incongruity and, as such, embraces the outsider, the unknown, the alien, and the estranged. The poetics of wrongness allies with anti-classicist movements like "Black is beautiful," camp, kitsch, the bizarre, the grotesque, the carnivalesque, the rococo, the Gurlesque, absurd, abject, macabre, surreal, uncanny, and with communities that have called their embodied poetics queer, crip, and mongrel.

In "Epilogue: Boarding the Voyage" (an essay added to *Voyage of the Sable Venus* after the first printing sold out) Robin Coste Lewis calls beauty "the greatest ideological territory of all." She also dedicates the book "to Beauty," but Lewis's beauty is not an ocular-centric subset of "rightness." "Beauty isn't pretty," writes Lewis in "Epilogue," "Beauty and pretty are enemies. Pretty is a Yes Man, dressed in colonial drag, passing for a lady. While Beauty is a double agent. Beauty is a war cry."

If capitalism depends on chattel slavery, what does beauty depend on? Who makes beauty? Who controls beauty? Who traffics in it? Who defines beauty and for what purpose? Who is harmed/oppressed/silenced by the production and commodification of beauty? What tools do artists use to dismantle oppressive beauty? The poetics of wrongness admires art and aesthetics that ask these questions, that enlarge, complicate, subvert, or mock a monolithic, monumental, hegemonic ideology of beauty, of pretty, of the "Yes Man, dressed in colonial drag."

Sorry (not sorry), Keats, beauty and truth are complicated and, more often than not, contradictory. Ye need to know that and so much more.

2. POETRY SHOULD BE SLANT.

Speaking of truth: there's another famous poet I'd like to contradict. "Tell all the truth but tell it slant," Emily Dickinson wrote, and she was wrong. Actually, the people who interpreted her directive to mean that poets should intentionally try to make the truth more obscure than it is —they are wrong.

> Tell all the truth but tell it slant —
> Success in Circuit lies
> Too bright for our infirm Delight
>
> The Truth's superb surprise
> As Lightning to the Children eased
> With explanation kind
> The Truth must dazzle gradually
> Or every man be blind —

The line "Tell all the truth but tell it slant" is almost always construed to mean that it is the poet's job to dole out truth in small doses or show the dimly lit world in flashes because telling a slant truth is kinder, less blinding, or because the slant truth is more interesting. This notion of slantness becomes a metonym for poetry itself, as if poetry is simply obscured, coded prose with weird formatting. (Truth + slant = poetry.) But the poetics of wrongness rejects this conception of poetry, rejects the way the infatuation with slantness has been used to bolster a poetics of coyness and indirection that often slips into glibness, abstraction, and meaninglessness.

I read Dickinson's short poem as a wittier, quieter, but no less powerful version of Jack Nicholson in *A Few Good Men* shouting, "You can't handle the truth!" or as a precursor to the lines in Muriel Rukeyser's poem "Käthe Kollwitz": "What would happen if one woman told the truth about her life? / The world would split open."

Dickinson isn't saying, "Don't tell all the truth." She's not even saying, "Don't tell it all at once." She's saying that the truth, unmediated and presented directly, will make human beings (or, perhaps, just men?) blind. Dickinson's use of the word "success" ("Success in Circuit lies") and the double meaning of "lies" contain a heavy dose of proto-irony[4]: one's success in being circuitous rather than direct might be kind but is also false.

All this is not to say the poetics of wrongness disavows Dickinson—far from it! I attribute the privileging of "slantness" as a poetic value not with Dickinson but, as I said before, a misunderstanding of Dickinson. There have been many helpful reconsiderations of Dickinson's work and life over the years. Adrienne Rich, for example, in her 1976 essay "Vesuvius at Home," pushes back against the way Dickinson's work was "narrowed-down by her early editors and anthologists, reduced to quaintness or spinsterish oddity by many of her commentators, sentimentalized, fallen-in-love with like some gnomic Garbo." Rich tries to imagine a Dickinson quite different from the one presented to Rich by anthologists and editors. Rich writes: "Emily Dickinson—viewed by her bemused

---

4. I heard Al Filreis use the term "proto-irony" to describe Dickinson in one of his ModPo conversations.

contemporary Thomas Higginson as 'partially cracked,' by the 20th century as fey or pathological—has increasingly struck me as a practical woman, exercising her gift as she had to, making choices. I have come to imagine her as somehow too strong for her environment, a figure of powerful will, not at all frail or breathless, someone whose personal dimensions would be felt in a household." Rich theorizes that Dickinson's isolation—chosen rather than imposed—may have been a practical solution for a woman who wanted to write rather than take care of children and a household.

Like all poets, Dickinson's formal choices and, particularly, her use of metaphor developed out of her circumstances, including her lived experience. I understand why Rich writes: "What [Dickinson] had to do was retranslate her own unorthodox, subversive, sometimes volcanic propensities into a dialect called metaphor: her native language. 'Tell all the Truth—but tell it Slant—.' It is always what is under pressure in us, especially under pressure of concealment—that explodes in poetry." Rich is rethinking the version of Dickinson as a mentally ill, hysterical, frail, celibate shut-in and seeing how a shift in this picture of Dickinson changes our reception of her poems. Rich posits that poetry is a place where "what is under pressure in us, especially under pressure of concealment," explodes. Rich wonders, in particular, about Dickinson's relationships with women and proposes that we "will understand Emily Dickinson better, read her poetry more perceptively, when the Freudian imputation of scandal and aberrance in women's love for women has been supplanted by a more informed, less misogynistic attitude toward women's experiences with each other." Rich's essay, which is just one voice in a vast chorus of responses to Dickinson, helps me place Dickinson's poems in the larger sociohistorical context of Dickinson's time and consider how the biases and assumptions of Dickinson's editors and critics may have affected my reading of Dickinson.[5]

It's also possible that Dickinson might *not* have been employing metaphor when she wrote, "The Truth must dazzle gradually / Or every man be blind," and that there is a more literal reading of this line that, until recently, has been largely ignored.

Poet and memoirist Stephen Kuusisto, interviewed by Ralph Savarese in *Journal of Literary & Cultural Disability Studies*, speaks about the relationship between disability and the lyric. Kuusisto mentions Dickinson in particular and the possibility that Dickinson's fear of going blind may have heightened "the brevity of the lyric impulse." Kuusisto explains:

> Emily Dickinson began to experience vision loss when she was in her thirties, and although we have no surviving medical notes about the matter we do know that she visited one of New England's leading ophthalmologists who examined her eyes with the newly invented ophthalmoscope. The doctor is said to have reassured her that she wasn't going blind. In turn, Emily Dickinson told her circle that she was not going blind. The odd thing is that after her visit to the eye doctor, she began to experience absolute photo-sensitivity—in effect she was blinded by daylight. Dickinson spent the remainder of her life living behind closed shutters, and she

5. While pondering Dickinson's use of the word "Circuit"—I wondered if Dickinson might mean circuit as in an electrical circuit (a complete path along which electricity can travel) as well as circuit as in "to go around"—I came across a 2003 article, "Domesticating Delphi: Emily Dickinson and the Electro-Magnetic Telegraph" by Jerusha Hull McCormack, that not only gave credence to this secondary meaning of "circuit," but made a compelling case that Dickinson's interest in the innovative technologies of her time, especially the telegraph and railroad, is key to understanding her style and meaning.

wouldn't even enter the main parlor of her family's house to greet visitors, preferring to speak with them from behind a half opened door. The available evidence suggests that she had a form of blindness that affects the rods and cones that process light—a form of blindness that her nineteenth-century eye doctor would not have seen by looking at her retinas with the opthalmoscope. I think that her poetry is thereafter concerned with interiority and with the evanescence of seeing—and that she works these things into lyrical studies of personal feeling and intuition. My general feeling is that Emily Dickinson was quite substantially visually impaired after 1862.

It's long been part of Dickinson lore that she was afraid of going blind, but this was often attributed to anxiety and hysteria. Rich interpreted "Tell all the Truth—but tell it Slant" as a metaphor for metaphoricity itself, a cipher of Dickinson's need to "retranslate her own unorthodox, subversive, sometimes volcanic propensities into a dialect called metaphor." Evidence of Dickinson's visual impairment was not available to Rich when she was writing about Dickinson in 1976. Disability Studies didn't begin to be taken seriously until the 1990s, and evidence of Dickinson's romantic, sexual, and literary relationship with Susan Huntington Gilbert Dickinson was overlooked and/or actively suppressed until the publication in 1998 of *Open Me Carefully*, edited by Ellen Louise Hart and Martha Nell Smith. The goal is not, however, to depose one reading for a "better" one. How might we continue to reimagine the meanings of Dickinson's line if we read it as simultaneously literal and figurative—if we reject any one, right reading?

The poetics of wrongness loves the multiple, inharmonious interpretations of this poem and all its volcanic propensities. The poetics of wrongness delights in slantness as a destabilizing, enlarging cosmology;

slant as an anti-singular, anti-exclusionary, anti-logocentric way of living, reading, writing, and being, because the poetics of wrongness is all for telling "all the truth" in all the ways, including (but never limited to) slant, slow, direct, brazen, lightning-fast, whispered, wailed, whined.

The poetics of wrongness does not abide the glorification of slantness if it leads to commandments about how one *should* "tell all the truth" or to a mandate of abstraction or who can/should tell their truth. The poetics of wrongness abhors admonitions and rules because these are habitually used as tools of domination, ways of *increasing* the pressure of concealment. The poetics of wrongness rejects slant = obscurity but reveres slant ≅ positionality. The poetics of wrongness celebrates slantness as a subversive/survivalist tool used by Dickinson and many other poets, especially poets who are not cishet white men. The poetics of wrongness cherishes embodied (rather than abstract) writing practices employed by poets who tell the truth of, about, and out of queer/disabled/racialized bodies.

I started this line of inquiry thinking I was going to end up with something like:

Poetry should be ~~slant~~.

I seem to have ended up in a place where the road sign reads:

Poetry ~~should~~ be slant *if* slant be [   ].

3. POETRY SHOULD BE SHORT.

Wrong. A poem should be as long as it needs to be.

The poems I love often brush up against the rules of the form, then run roughshod over those rules, then turn around and spit in their face.

It's not that a short poem is *necessarily* impossible, but the poetics of wrongness rejects the notion that what makes a poem a poem is that it contains language that is best or better than regular language (see anti-tenet #1) or is a thing of beauty made with language (see anti-tenet #1) or that it is a difficult, tricky, obscured truth for the sake of inventiveness or kindness to the reader (see anti-tenet #2) or that what distinguishes poetry from other forms of language is brevity, concision, not an extra word in sight.

Here's a tiny, lovely poem by W. S. Merwin:

SEPARATION

Your absence has gone through me
Like thread through a needle.
Everything I do is stitched with its color.

Here's another short poem, this one by Margaret Atwood, less sweet but also powerful:

YOU FIT INTO ME

you fit into me
like a hook into an eye

a fish hook
an open eye

And, perhaps my favorite short poem: "Poetry" by Marianne Moore:

POETRY

I, too, dislike it.
    Reading it, however, with a perfect contempt for it, one discovers in
    it, after all, a place for the genuine.

The poetics of wrongness can admire poems which have a remarkable ability to surprise and confuse and contradict in a small space. Moore's contempt isn't "perfect," of course; it has a fault in which the appeal of poetry slips through. She makes space for the genuine in her poem in part by contradicting herself and by undercutting our assumptions of what poetry should be. This poem is called "Poetry" but doesn't sound or look very much like a lyric poem. It feels more like an aphorism or the moral at the end of a fable or a riddle than a poem, and it's not quite clear (despite the cheeky simplicity of the first line) what exactly she dislikes about poetry, how reading with contempt allows for the discovery of the genuine, or what she even means by "genuine" in terms of an attribute for poetry.

What I like about the poem is that it sounds demotic and self-assured—the voice of a wise and seasoned poet-teacher—but fails in its definition and legibility in compelling ways. "Poetry" may seem to be a simple, dashed-off opinion, but the poem was revised several times over several decades. The version above (the shortest of the versions) was the one Moore chose for *The Complete Poems of Marianne Moore* (1967). I love that this poem thumbs its nose at critics and readers who had admiringly commented on the earlier (longer) versions, especially the 1924 version, which contains one of Moore's most quoted lines: "imaginary gardens with real toads." The longer version of "Poetry" is wild but meticulous and contains a bat, elephants, a wolf, a strange simile ("the immovable critic twitching his skin like a horse that feels a flea"), a baseball fan, statistician, several more jibes at literary critics, a quotation from William Butler Yeats ("literalists of the imagination") which was Yeats's light criticism of William Blake, and these amazing last lines:

> In the meantime, if you demand on the one hand,
>   the raw material of poetry in
>   all its rawness and
>   that which is on the other hand
>   genuine, you are interested in poetry.

In an article about Moore's revisions of "Poetry," Robert Pinsky writes, "Moore, as I understand her project, champions both clarity and complexity, rejecting the shallow notion that they are opposites." I agree, and I understand Moore's decision to include the 1924 version (widely considered to be the best version) as an endnote to the three-line version (widely considered to be the worst) in her *Complete Poems* as a sort of clever but serious joke. If you are really interested in poetry, you will demand both "the raw material of poetry in / all its rawness" *and* "that which is on the other hand / genuine." Moore admonishes: If you are interested in poetry, you will not worship concision or any other poetic device. You will not slavishly pursue a single, reducible, easy definition of what poetry is. Especially when read in relation to the longer versions of the poem, I do not see "Poetry" as promoting short poems, but rather as implicating itself, as a poem, as part of what one dislikes but still engages in, as an effort to get at something wild, complex, raw, and genuine.

I reject shortness as a goal. The poetics of wrongness does not adore Occam's razor, or the law of parsimony: poems are not problems to be solved with the fewest possible words. Length as a standard of measure for poetry is irrelevant, but, if it matters at all, I would say that it is *more* difficult for short poems to embody a poetics of wrongness.

See how well-behaved those poems are? How easily I can insert them into this lecture, how easily you can sigh a self-satisfied "poetry sigh" and move on? They are portable, easily memorizable. They are digestible and, often, feel predigested. And these are the good ones. Many short poems read to me as self-satisfied products of a condescending mind. The poet, like a parent bird, has chewed up the world and regurgitated it into my open beak or has come at me with a thin needle, promising to painlessly insert the essence of something into my bloodstream. Get away from me, lyric poet of beauty and perfection! Give me, instead, food with all its fiber. Give me a poem that has the grit and pebbles necessary to break down a whole disgusting, moving worm. The poetics of wrongness prefers real foods even if they make me sick, even when I have to chew and chew and chew.

The poetics of wrongness doesn't want a chiseled jewel or a small purse of emotions recollected in tranquility. The poetics of wrongness wants the kind of poetry that, as Sylvia Plath said, "at its best can do you a lot of harm." Of course it can harm: "The blood jet is poetry, / There is no stopping it" (as Plath herself wrote).

I want Bernadette Mayer's unwieldy, book-length, 150-page poem, *Midwinter Day,* that she supposedly (it is impossible) wrote all in one day, a book that travels from dreams to consciousness and back, that includes the voices of her children, the history of her town, sex, what she eats for lunch, gossip, lines in Shakespearean meter, prose, and common lists.

Mayer writes: "The history of every historical thing including God but not including all men and women individually, is a violent mess like this ice. But for the spaces even hunchbacked history has allowed in between the famous and loud for something that's defined as what does please us. Which is perhaps the story of an intimate family, though you won't believe or will be unable to love it, driven to research love's limits in its present solitude as if each man or woman in the world was only one person with everything I've mentioned separate in him or she didn't represent any history at all though he or she had stories to tell and was just sitting kind of crazily before an open window in midwinter . . ."

How else can Mayer begin to accurately describe the incoherence of the mind, of life, being a woman, being alive? This poem is *impossible* and feels nearly unstoppable, and she does it successfully by including her awareness of the inherent failure of the project.

Instead of the Fabergé egg of a short lyric, the poetics of wrongness prefers the aesthetics of intractability and exhaustive exhaustedness, the physicality and ruptured rapture, the unapologetic plainspokenness of James Schuyler's long poems, such as "Hymn to Life," "The Morning of the Poem," and "A few days," that are too long and messy and loose to be poems, but are poems nonetheless. His lines are too long for the page, too long to scan, too long to function as standalone lines, but they are, most certainly, lines of poetry. His tally of physical complaints, his observations about garbage trucks and air conditioners are anti-poetic and embraced and lauded by the poetics of wrongness.

I want the book-length poem *Tape for the Turn of the Year* by A. R. Ammons, in which he typed (and did not later edit) a poem that begins and ends at a length determined by a two-and-a-quarter-inch-wide roll of adding-machine paper that would turn out to be two hundred pages long. Ammons loves and hates the roll of paper, adores and despises the project. The poem is so long his back suffers. The project is like a long marriage and provides him ample opportunity to be wrong, to change his mind, and find himself again and again. It is epic and anti-epic.

Odysseus is a man trying to get home; Ammons is a man who almost never leaves home. (The few times he leaves home for more than a few hours during the five weeks or so of composing, Ammons carries his typewriter with the roll of tape inside it along with him.) He must continue the poem until the roll runs out. He is Penelope at her loom, but never unweaving, and it is the moments when Ammons grows exasperated, exhausted, bored that he comes upon exquisite language-making. Thank goodness he did not edit this poem down to the crucial plot points or a greatest-hits collection of best lines. It is the discursive, rambling journey of this poem and its many mistakes that are its glory.

What do you get when you mix the pursuits of brevity and beauty? Advertising. The motto, the jingle, the political slogan. A pitch that should take no longer than a ride in an elevator. The poetics of wrongness prefers the stairs, prefers a half-finished, crumbling stairway to nowhere. The poetics of wrongness often can't fit in an elevator, wouldn't know what button to press, doesn't know where it's going, suffers from a fear of elevators, and has forgotten its keys and wallet. The poetics of wrongness wants poems that are expansive, inclusive, contradictory, self-conscious, ashamed, irreverent. It's hard to be those things in one hundred words or less.

What, you might ask, is the advantage of this ongoingness, this going-on-and-onness? I don't have time for all this meandering, you might say. I find long-windedness inconsiderate and annoying.

Well, first of all, the poetics of wrongness prefers poems that some people worship and other people detest to poems that everyone "likes," so your dislike does not worry me. Second, one note does not music make. Third, the poetics of wrongness values process over product, and longer poems are almost always more honest and self-conscious about their status as made things than short poems, in that long poems are often self-aware of their own making.

I'm not saying that longer is always or inherently better. The poetics of wrongness is not interested in who can eat the most hot dogs without throwing up or who can hold her breath underwater for the longest time. The poetics of wrongness likes a good rant or jeremiad but disdains the filibuster. It's not length for length's sake that I appreciate. Let us not hold longness up as the new beauty!

A bad poem that goes on for a long time is surely worse than if it were quickly over. It's not length that makes something good, but there is something about the presence of time in a poem that pleases the poetics of wrongness and something about the sleight-of-hand, refined, sublimed, edited nature of many short poems makes the poetics of wrongness (or at least this poet of wrongness) cringe.

The very long or book-length poems I've mentioned take time and are about time, and in the time that it takes to write these poems, the poet punches a time card into the time clock of the poem and begins to become real (to the reader and to herself) in a different way. There is space (created by time)—can you see my son rolling his eyes at my misuse of physics?—for the poet to inhabit, for the reader too.

When one sees a painting by Jackson Pollock, one might notice color and composition, but the thrill of these paintings is the way in which the viewer sees a record of Pollock's body moving through time and space as he splattered or threw paint. Made works are records of an artist's time, but some are more conspicuous in their recording of this time or in their preoccupation with time. Some art goes to great lengths to pretend that it emerged fully formed, like Athena from the forehead of Zeus. The poetics of wrongness is not interested in art made by the gods or by God and gives no gold star for the illusion of effortlessness.

Perhaps you say it is boring to watch a person sit in a chair hour after hour, day after day, breathing in and out and in and out, taking breaks to eat and shit and make love and listen to the weather. You say this is not what art should be about or what art is for.

The poetics of wrongness cares not for an absent God-artist we can't see or hear, but wants the living miracle of a real-person-in-a-real-place-at-a-real-time.

The poetics of wrongness says that art *is* these moments of repetition and recurrence and that in the time it takes to read such a long poem—in the experiential recognition of how long it took to write such a poem—the poet becomes real. With frustration and boredom and anger, with familiarity and adoration and gratitude, the writer and reader spend time together. The poem is their meeting place—the place where they become visible to each other and begin to have a relationship that is both imaginary and real, full of faults and failure and desire.

4. POETRY SHOULD BE TIMELESS.

Speaking of time, the poetics of wrongness has a problem with "timelessness" as a virtue.

A journalist once said to me, "Journalism is important to a large number of people for a very short period of time, whereas poetry is important to a few people for (potentially) a long period of time." OK, maybe. But this does not necessarily lead to the widely held belief that a good poem should be "timeless."

I've already said that being full of time, visibly, audibly, palpably full of time, can be an asset, and I know that "timeless" is not meant to imply "without time"—most poems have some relationship to narrative, and narrativity cannot exist without time—but the poetics of wrongness rejects "timelessness" and lastingness as essential poetic attributes and suggests "timeliness" as an alternative.

The poetics of wrongness wants a poetry that is conscious of time (time-full), that is of a particular time (timely), and that is relevant (timely). Some poems will last and continue to be relevant, but the poetics of wrongness wants a poem that is hard to capture and hard to hold. The poetics of wrongness wants a poem that will *not* last forever because it is fresh, alive, unstable, potentially (hopefully) useful at a *now* moment even if sometimes the poem is on its deathbed. The poetics of wrongness is not afraid of hospice. Everything alive dies. Everything fresh expires. The poetics of wrongness wants poems with a shelf life, made with living ingredients.

The poetics of wrongness would like artists to rethink the idea that the purpose of making art is to make something that will outlive and outlast our minor, mortal lives. Rethink the goal of making something that will *endure*. Rethink the virtue of timelessness. Do you want to write a poem that will outlive you? That will last forever? Really? Like plastic? Like toxic waste?

5. POETRY SHOULD BE UNIVERSAL.

As far as I can tell, my students' strongly held belief that poems *must* be about universal subjects and/or be written from a universal perspective and/or appeal to a universal audience comes from their teachers, who got it from their teachers, who got it from their teachers, going way back to a misunderstanding of a mistranslation of a few taken-out-of-context lines of Aristotle's *Poetics* in which Aristotle sets up a pissing contest between history and poetry and declares poetry the winner. This edict to write universal poems is, at best, bad advice. It's confusing, paradoxical, and sinister and often results in a lowest-common-denominator poetics of abstraction in which everyone is equally estranged from meaning.

Here are a few universal (i.e., widely shared) experiences that my students almost never write about: academic pressure, pooping, masturbating, homesickness and/or the complications of living at home, sibling rivalry/love, grief when someone they love dies. They rarely write directly about these nearly universal experiences because they consider them too common—banal, vulgar, boring, unexceptional—for poetry. Common experiences are worthy of poetry only if they are traumatic, superlative, overtly political, or symbolic of something uncommon. So, students mine their personal lives for the very worst thing that's ever happened to them. Others write poems in which they metaphorize tragic events that have not happened to them. Some write in the voice of a real or imagined famous/infamous person. Or, not wanting to risk being accused of narcissism, trauma porn, appropriation, being blind to their own privilege, being boring, exoticizing themselves, or playing the "race card" or "victim card," some students reject narrativity altogether and use experimental formal devices that distract from the commonness of the subject matter or become the poem's only legible subject matter.

My students are smart. They've been raised in a culture of American exceptionalism that worships celebrity and is deeply exclusionary. They know they're too brown or black, too poor, female, queer, atypical, and too common to be Everyman.

32

"I celebrate myself, and sing myself," begins Walt Whitman's "Song of Myself." "And what I assume you shall assume, / For every atom belonging to me as good belongs to you." To love Whitman for being an Everyman who loves everything and everyone, to call Whitman's invocation of everything in the universe "universal," "democratic," or "inclusive" willfully ignores Whitman's racist, colonialist language and rhetoric. To love Whitman's cataloguing, directness, loudness, corporality, ego, and expansiveness because it is universal is to misconstrue Whitman's work and the contemporary American formulation of universalism.

In *Citizen: An American Lyric*, poet Claudia Rankine writes:

> A friend argues that Americans battle between the "historical self" and the "self self." By this she means you mostly interact as friends with mutual interest and, for the most part, compatible personalities; however, sometimes your historical selves, her white self and your black self, or your white self and her black self, arrive with the full force of your American positioning.

Is there a "self self," a "self" outside of history? Is there an "authentic" self? A "singular" self? A "real," "true" self? I think a lot, care a lot about these questions. I've written about or out of these questions since I started writing. It's quite a common obsession with poets.

"Is 'I' even me or am 'I' a gearshift to get from one sentence to the next? Should I say we? Is the voice not various if I take responsibility for it? What does my subject mean to me?" Rankine asks in *Don't Let Me Be Lonely: An American Lyric*.

Twenty years ago, I would have said, on most days, that I believe there is an authentic self, an "I" that exists outside of culture and history. More recently, I'd likely say the self is always historical, always constructed. The more I study philosophy, psychology, epistemology, and metaphysics, the less certain I am of either answer, of any one answer. Of any singular, right definition of "I" that is anything more than "a gearshift to get from one sentence to the next."

The poetics of wrongness is deeply, increasingly suspicious of universality as the brass ring for which *all* poets and poems *should* reach. Insisting poets write about common experiences that "everyone" can relate to but expecting them to write only about male, white, heterosexual, cis, "normative" experiences that according to straight cis white men are "universal" is a weaponized scam of white supremacy, settler colonialism, and the cishet patriarchy.

The poetics of wrongness rails against the way in which universalism is used to exclude minoritized bodies or subjects or tones from poetry. The poetics of wrongness prefers, instead, to write out of and about difference, to write from the peculiar, personal, specific parts of our brains, bodies, and souls that are broken, disrupted, and atypical. Write out of your fetishes and aphasias, if you have them. Write the most specific, honest portrayal of your most peculiar, obscene, esoteric quality. Or don't!

"Poetry is a mirror which makes beautiful that which is distorted," wrote Percy Bysshe Shelley. The poetry of wrongness would like to try to describe the distorted and the distortion without making it beautiful. "Pain is filtered in a poem so that it becomes finally, in the end, pleasure," according to Mark Strand. The poetics of wrongness would like a pain that stays pain not because this is a poetics of sadomasochism (although the poetics of wrongness has no problem with sadomasochism) but because it is a poetics of what is, not what would be nice, and certainly not what is considered nice/best/normal/universal by those in power.

Even if I were able to rescue universality from its highly problematic history and its tendency to mean "majority" or "mainstream," even if I could forgive the social utopianism that underlies the snake oil of color-blindness and similar universalist myths, I still reject universalism. Even if your atoms and mine are remarkably similar, even if we are all made of what everything in the cosmos is made up of, let me *not* assume I *am you*. Let me not universalize (literally "turn into one"). Let me not assume I know you or what kind of poems you should write or not write.

Here is the end of Alice Notley's long poem "The Prophet":

> Do not generally
> Go about giving advice. That which is everybody's business
>   is nobody's
> Business. Let thyself become undeceived through the
>   beauty & strangeness of
> The physical world. It is almost possible to believe that if you
>   look at it really see it be it for yourself
> You will be free. They say it will be cloudy tomorrow but they
> Are often wrong. There's a lot to say about two & one. Your life
> Is not small or mean, it is beautiful & big, full of
>   planets clouds skies and
> Also your tiniest things of you. One is you & all this & two & yet.
>   You must never
> Stop making jokes. You are not great you are life.

By all means, write what is common, what belongs to all, what is "owned or used jointly," what is "general, of a public nature." By all and any means, write in your common, vulgar, familiar language of common, vulgar, familiar things. Write, write, write, for "there's a lot to say about two & one." As Robin Coste Lewis says: "I write because life is lonely and I want you there." Use "I," whoever and whatever she is, to help you get from one sentence to another. Let "I" acknowledge personal and institutional bias rather than selling the snake oil of colorblindness and other universalist myths. Let "I" be one "& two & yet" as "I" reaches out to you and you and you and you. Remember: "They say it will be cloudy tomorrow but they / Are often wrong." Remember, the poetics of wrongness loves "your tiniest things of you."

6. POETRY IS CLOSE TO GODLINESS.

The poetics of wrongness is anthropocentric: It is written by human beings for human beings and about human beings. It is interested in the divine and nature as seen and experienced through the human senses and intellect.

In its preference for the literal, for the direct, for the domestic, for the political, for the relational, for the sociological, for the individual, for the particular, the poetics of wrongness can be perceived as atheist. This is not necessarily the case. The poetics of wrongness knows that ideology is a petri dish for wrongness. The poetics of wrongness is foundationally antifundamentalist even though being anti-anything can easily develop into fundamentalism.

The poetics of wrongness recognizes prayer as an ancient and enduring form of writing out of wrongness, both external and internal. The poetics of wrongness loves the impossibility of monotheism but only for its impossibility and for the ways in which it reveals the fragility and pathos and imagination and terror of humankind.

The poetics of wrongness knows that whoever or whatever or however created the world, it wasn't by my own hand, and I have only the power to name and love and suffer and die. If the poetics of wrongness believes in any God, it is a God of Human Failure, a God imagined to make visible in us all that is ungodly: doubt, weakness, fallibility, fear, ineptitude, physicality, mortality. The poetics of wrongness is interested in getting close to God (or beauty or perfection) only insofar as the journey reveals the inherent and absolute failure of our inevitable reaching.

As Whitman said:

Why should I wish to see God better than this day?
I see something of God each hour of the twenty-four, and each moment
    then,
In the faces of men and women I see God, and in my own face in the glass,
I find letters from God dropt in the street, and every one is sign'd by God's
    name,
And I leave them where they are, for I know that wheresoe'er I go,
Others will punctually come for ever and ever.

Or, they will not. Perhaps we will finally destroy the world one day; in which case, let us be thankful that we made poetry and had poetry.

FINAL THOUGHTS

It is by misunderstanding these poets and these ideas about poetry and by feeling misunderstood by them that I have come to have the courage and energy to say anything at all.

I've spent most of my life figuring out who I want to be by figuring out how to be unlike (and like) my mother. I watch my sons come into adulthood, wanting to do things their own way, which arises out of an awareness of my wrongness, my insufficiency, and which also arises out of their awareness of who I am or who they think I am. My husband and I hurt each other as we struggle to see one another as separate and connected, to apprehend each other with honesty and kindness.

Human babies are astonishingly dependent and remain so for an impossibly long period of time. It is remarkable how long it takes for infants to perceive that they are not one with the universe, not at one with the face that is (hopefully) staring back at them with love. Oppositionality is not always an act of violence or hatred to the one opposed; it is often an act of differentiation, which is a normal and natural part of being a responsible and connected human being.

"Poetry," wrote Allen Ginsberg, "is not an expression of the party line. It's that time of night, lying in bed, thinking what you really think, making the private world public, that's what the poet does." The poetics of wrongness agrees! Part of knowing what I think is knowing what I do not agree with, saying NO to the party line. And, making our private disagreements public? Yes, that's what the poet does.

So, what if there were no more "party line"? Would poetry cease to exist? Cease to be necessary? I say that such an age of agreement and sameness and rightness will never come to be and that, therefore, poetry will always be necessary.

Of course, I would love to be proven wrong.

WHAT WE TALK ABOUT WHEN WE TALK ABOUT THE CONFESSIONAL AND WHAT WE SHOULD BE TALKING ABOUT

In late January 2013, I told my mother I was going to publish my memoir, called *MOTHERs*, despite the fact that she'd told me she did not want me to and that, if I did, terrible things would happen to her, to me, and to my children. A few hours after receiving my email and forwarding it to several friends with a note saying that I was breaking her heart, my mother, who was in Taiwan at the time, was rushed to the hospital. She suffered an aortic dissection and never regained consciousness after an emergency heart-valve replacement surgery.

For months after my mother's death, I organized memorials, cleaned out her apartment, managed her literary estate, and mourned her, all while feeling and believing that I'd killed her, that my actions—my writing and my decision to publish that writing—had in small or large ways precipitated her sudden death. I stopped writing. Perhaps I was in shock or afraid of my own writing or perhaps I imagined that never writing again was penance.

Two years after my mother's death I began to write the lectures that would eventually become the essays in this book. I started reading and writing about two topics: photography and confessional poetry. When I completed drafts of these two lectures I realized that they were both about my mother's death, although neither of them mentioned her directly. I'd written about the similarities and differences between photography and poetry and about how my interest in photography had led me to privilege documentary poetry or poetry with a social purpose. I'd written about the way confessional poetry breaks rules, subverts norms, violates privacy, provokes, and offends, and about the angry, uncomfortable responses of critics and certain readers to this kind of poetry. I wrote a third lecture about all the ways my writing has hurt others. I made a list of everything I'd written that hurt someone, my most provocative and offensive poems and lines.

In retrospect—it is so clear *now*—I was trying to exculpate myself. I was searching for antecedents and justifications for my practice of writing accessible, autobiographical poems and prose about my mental/emotional state, my body, and my lived experience and for including, in that writing, real people—my children, my husband, my friends, other poets—whom I named or otherwise identified, with or without their consent. I was trying to align myself with like-minded artists and artistic movements in order to find protection and permission for the way my poems mimic photography's relationship to "the real" and the way my poems rely on the excitement and/or discomfort of revealing "too much."

Given the subject matter, I want to acknowledge directly and up front what was and is at stake for me in the investigation of the history and legacy of the confessional impulse. I want to admit that I reread the confessional poets and rethought the legacy of these poets in order to consider, for myself, whether my practice of "flouting decorum" and writing "in a way that interrogates what it means to tell the truth" in the style of Plath and Olds makes me "a courageous poet," a rude, excessive, depressive poet, or a murderer.

Even before the crisis of my mother's death, I had come to feel that as a poet, particularly as a woman poet, I was trapped in an increasingly confining room and that the doors out of that room were each differently problematic. To write primarily about myself was narcissistic, self-indulgent, privileged, and hysterical. To write about others (both living and dead) meant I was likely to hurt the person or people about whom I was writing. To write as someone else (as in a persona poem) or to tell stories that were not part of my own lived experience raised questions of appropriation. In order to assess the consequences of opening the confessional, I needed to figure out, for myself, what that word even meant.

A great deal has been written about Robert Lowell, John Berryman, W. D. Snodgrass, Sylvia Plath, and Anne Sexton. This is not an in-depth analysis of any of their work, nor is it a thorough exploration of any of their lives. I invoke and explore their work and lives and the critical response to their lives from an extremely self-centered position. I write about Lowell, Plath, Sexton, and Allen Ginsberg in order to explore what it means to be called a confessional poet today. How is the term used/misused? What is the origin of the term? Is "confessional" a useful term, a term I want to reclaim? Or is the term like a muddy smudge on the lens, a veiled (often misogynist) criticism that obscures more useful ways of talking about poetry?

Like most literary movements or schools, confessional poetry contains unlikely bedfellows. In this case, none of the original confessional poets wanted to be called confessional, and each of these poets wrote in a range of styles and modes across their writing lives. That said, rereading the work of Lowell, Snodgrass, Berryman, Sexton, and Plath and the criticism of the period in an attempt at taxonomy, I was able to locate several common attributes.

Poems that are called confessional rely heavily on sound and repetition, use simple syntax, remark on the passage of time, and are less interested in compression than most lyric poems. These poems tend to be narrative, are relatively accessible, and often include a mix of verse and prose. They are emotionally shrill, self-absorbed, hysterical, messy, and traffic in shame. They tend to be long, are often written in series, have a strong awareness of audience, and are preoccupied with religion. Many poems by these original confessional poets are written by non-Jews about Judaism or Jewish history and have a particular fascination with the Holocaust.

Some so-called confessional poems contain most of these attributes, others very few. Part of the confusion around the term is that it originally referred specifically to these five poets and specifically to the poems they were writing in the late 1950s and early 1960s, but the term "confessional" quickly began to be used to describe a mode, a style, a quality of poems written by many poets across several decades.[1] If that were not complicated enough, when Sylvia Plath and Anne Sexton's poems gained readership and popularity, "confessional" more and more became an epithet critics leveled against poets and poems as a sexist (and later racist and heterocentrist) gatekeeping strategy.

1. The word "lyric" is similarly slippery—is "lyric" a quality, a category, a genre, a strategy? Is the lyricism of a poem willed by the poet, assigned by critics (or bookstores), or located in the relationship between the poem and the reader?

No one has ever compared me to Lowell, Snodgrass, or Berryman, and I'd say my poems are much more like Sexton's than like Plath's. When critic Craig Morgan Teicher said in his review of my third book, *The Bad Wife Handbook*, that I was heir to Plath, Glück, and Olds, I believe he wasn't really comparing my poems to Plath's but was suggesting, rather, that I am heir to Plath's *confessional legacy*, which has more to do with accessibility, truth-telling, emotional volume, self-absorption, hysteria, sloppiness, and speed than with the forms or poetic practices of Plath's (or Glück's or Olds's) poems.

So, if the term is so confusing and problematic, why not simply retire it the way we have thankfully retired "poetess"? The thing is, to disavow the term altogether is to overlook the extent to which contemporary poets, myself included, are profoundly influenced by the legacy of confessional writing and the extent to which we, who are both drawn to and repelled by this legacy, are in need of a poetry that employs elements of what is often called confessional. Examining the origin and evolution of the term "confessional" also helps to illuminate the continued misogyny of the critical reception of poets like Sharon Olds and continued erasure and/or ghettoizing of poets who are anything other than white heterosexual cis men.

■ ■ ■

The term "confessional" as it relates to poetry was coined by critic M. L. Rosenthal in "Poetry as Confession," his 1959 review of Robert Lowell's book *Life Studies*. Rosenthal's review begins: "Emily Dickinson once called publication 'the auction of the mind.' Robert Lowell seems to regard it more as soul's therapy."

Is it Rosenthal's thinly veiled, somewhat uncertain opinion that Lowell should not have published *Life Studies*? Emily Dickinson famously did not publish her poems, and although the reasons for this and the circumstances surrounding Dickinson's seclusion have long been debated, Rosenthal's invocation of Dickinson's lines, "Publication — is the Auction / Of the Mind of Man —" implies that publication, especially the publication of a certain kind of material, is the act of making public what should be private and of profiting (either to become richer or to escape debt) from that which cannot be and should not be commodified. In the Dickinson poem to which Rosenthal refers, Dickinson goes on to call publication "so foul a thing." The foul act of publication is possibly justified by poverty, Dickinson admits, but short of extreme need (and perhaps even in the face of extreme poverty), Dickinson advises that "We" should prefer death ("From Our Garret go / White — unto the White Creator —") rather than "be the Merchant / Of the Heavenly Grace." We should do anything possible so as to "reduce no Human Spirit / To Disgrace of Price —" writes Dickinson. Rosenthal suggests that publication as "soul's therapy" involves a similar "disgrace" and wonders, throughout the review, about the damage wrought by this disgrace.

Rosenthal is not suggesting that Lowell is the first or only poet to regard poetry as "soul's therapy." But something about the way Robert Lowell was using poetry or the fact that Lowell, specifically, was engaging in this use of poetry as soul's therapy concerned Rosenthal greatly. His review continues:

> The use of poetry for the most naked kind of confession grows apace in our day. We are now far from the great Romantics who, it is true, spoke directly of their emotions but did not give the game away even to themselves. They found, instead, cosmic equations and symbols, transcenden-

tal reconciliations . . . in the course of which . . . the poet lost his personal complaint in the music of universal forlornness. Later, Whitman took American poetry to the very edge of the confessional in his *Calamus* poems and in the quivering avowal of his helplessness before the seductions of 'blind loving wrestling touch, sheath'd hooded sharp-tooth'd touch.' More recently, under the influence of the Symbolists, Eliot and Pound brought us into the forbidden realm itself, yet even in their work a certain indirection masks the poet's actual face and psyche from greedy eyes.

Lowell removes the mask. His speaker is unequivocally himself, and it is hard not to think of *Life Studies* as a series of personal confidences, rather shameful, that one is honor-bound not to reveal.

Poets had always written about feelings; this was not new. The Romantic poets had big feelings about which they spoke directly, but the Romantic poet, through his use of symbols and "transcendental reconciliations," managed to lose "his personal complaint in the music of universal forlornness." Whitman "took us to the very edge of the confessional," explains Rosenthal, who makes "the confessional" sound a lot like the forbidden fruit of the tree of knowledge or the unknown interior of Pandora's box. Luckily (for whom?), Whitman, despite being gravely seduced (and seducing?), stays at the edge. Eliot and Pound, according to Rosenthal, "brought us into the forbidden realm itself"—Danger! Danger!—"yet even in their work a certain indirection masks the poet's actual face and psyche from greedy eyes."[2] Coming as we are, almost sixty

2. Here, Rosenthal doubly invokes "psyche." He is saying that indirection is necessary to protect a poet's face (identity and also self-respect, as in "save face") and psyche (soul, spirit, ego). But he is also invoking the myth of Psyche and Eros. Psyche, harassed and bullied by her jealous older sisters, develops an insatiable curiosity to see the face of her lover and, violating his emphatic instructions, lights a postcoital candle to gaze upon his sleeping face. At this moment she sees his divine beauty, which

45

years after these words were written and after sixty years of poetry inspired in part by the very thing Rosenthal is noticing, it may be difficult for us to understand Rosenthal's alarm and his preference for masks, indirection, sublimation, and losing one's personal complaint in universal forlornness.

M. L. (Macha) Rosenthal (called "Mack" by his friends) was born in March 1917 in Washington, DC, to Jewish immigrant parents who spoke Yiddish at home. His parents divorced when he was young, and, after the divorce, his father became Orthodox. Rosenthal moved frequently in his youth and lived mostly with his mother and stepfather. According to his *New York Times* obituary, Rosenthal said that his interest in poetry began at an early age. "My father gave us kids a nickel every time we recited a poem. A poet who was a friend of his one day told him: 'You mustn't do that. They'll grow up thinking there is money in poetry.'" Rosenthal became a poet, critic, editor, and professor. His specialty was modern poetry, especially the poetry of Yeats, Pound, Eliot, and William Carlos Williams, and he made his living by writing about poetry and from teaching poetry, including teaching for over fifty years at New York University. In addition to publishing six poetry collections of his own, Rosenthal served as poetry editor at *The Nation*, *Present Tense*, and *The Humanist*, wrote reviews and critical introductions, and edited some of the most influential anthologies and readers of his time, including *The*

---

she had known but not trusted, and recognizes him as the god of love. A hot drop of oil spills upon the god, and he is incensed at this violation and flies off, leaving Psyche to atone for her misdeeds by performing a series of trials. The very meaning of our Western concept of "soul" is connected to our understanding of the relationship between curiosity, the desire to "see" or know, privacy, trust, betrayal, and love.

New Poets: American and British Poets and *Chief Modern Poets of England and America.*[3]

Robert Traill Spence Lowell IV (often called "Cal") was born the same month and year into a prominent Boston family "that could trace its origins back to the *Mayflower*." Through his father, Lowell was related to famous war heroes, clergymen, judges, and poets. On his mother's side, he was related to William Samuel Johnson, who signed the Constitution of the United States, Calvinist theologian Jonathan Edwards, Puritan reformer Anne Hutchinson, early New York colonist Robert Livingston, and several other famous New Englanders.

When Rosenthal wrote "Poetry as Confession," Lowell was already a famous poet and very much the heir apparent of modernist poetry. This destiny was sometimes self-proclaimed, as evidenced by Lowell's rather immodest letter to Ezra Pound, which Lowell wrote as an undergraduate at Harvard, and which contains the following sentences:

> I would like to bring back momentum and movement in poetry on a grand scale, to master your tremendous machinery and to carry your standard further into the century; and I think I have life enough to withstand the years of pounding and grinding before accomplishment.

Such grandiosity may have been an early sign of Lowell's mania, but Lowell had been called a genius from a young age and was encouraged in his poetic endeavors and supported in his pursuits. When Lowell was

---

3. Growing up, I remember looking through my father's edition of *Chief Modern Poets*. The reddish cover of volume 2, *The American Poets*, was faded, and the interior much underlined. The table of contents suggested to me that these were the only American poets. My father is not the only Ivy League–educated man of his generation whose poetry education ended with Robert Lowell.

unhappy at Harvard, a psychiatrist (who was also a poet) suggested he visit the poet Allen Tate. Lowell did so, staying with Tate and his wife for two months, and then followed Tate to Kenyon, where Lowell met Randall Jarrell and completed his undergraduate degree in classics.

Lowell won the Pulitzer Prize in 1947, at age thirty, for his second book, *Lord Weary's Castle*. T. S. Eliot and William Carlos Williams both praised the book, and John Berryman, in a review of *Lord Weary's Castle*, described Lowell as "a talent whose ceiling is invisible." Of *Lord Weary's Castle*, Randall Jarrell predicted: "one or two of these poems will be read as long as men remember English." From 1947–1948, Lowell served as poet laureate[4], and in the early 1950s Lowell taught at the Iowa Writers' Workshop (where he taught W. D. Snodgrass) and later at Boston University (where he taught Anne Sexton and Sylvia Plath).

Between the publication of *Lord Weary's Castle* and *Life Studies* Lowell divorced Jean Stafford (1948) and married Elizabeth Hardwick (1949). Lowell's father died in 1950, his mother died in 1954, and Lowell was institutionalized many times for bipolar disorder, including three weeks in a locked ward at a mental hospital in New York (1954). Lowell's daughter, Harriet, was born in 1957.

Lowell's third book, *The Mills of the Kavanaughs* (1951), did not garner the same praise as his earlier books. In his 2003 review of Lowell's *Collected Poems* (edited by Frank Bidart) James Longenbach describes "The Mills of the Kavanaughs" as "the long poem standing between the New Critical Lowell of *Lord Weary's Castle* and the confessional Lowell of *Life Studies*." Longenbach believes that Lowell's "struggle to remake

4. At the time, the position was called Consultant in Poetry to the Library of Congress.

himself in the years leading up to *Life Studies*" was mostly unknown to "early readers [who] were at liberty to perceive this book as a strategic rejection of the traditional values of T. S. Eliot and Allen Tate." It certainly makes sense to me that a man who had experienced all that Lowell had between 1946 and 1959 was trying to remake himself (and save himself) as much as or more than he was rejecting Eliot and Tate. In fact, Lowell's therapist explicitly suggested that Lowell write about his early life, and this resulted in the long prose memoir, "91 Revere Street," that comprises the second section of *Life Studies*.

What happens, then, according to Rosenthal, when Lowell removes the mask and is "unequivocally himself"? "About half the book," Rosenthal writes, "is essentially a public discrediting of his father's manliness and character, as well as of the family and social milieu of his childhood." We hear about "the poet's psychological problems as an adult" and spy "grotesque glimpses into his marital life."

When Rosenthal wrote, "Lowell seems to regard [poetry] . . . as soul's therapy," he was remarking on something new in Lowell and in poetry. Lowell was disobeying his inherited Boston Brahmin mandate to be discreet and inconspicuous and was defying the tradition of modern poetry which he had previously exemplified. Perhaps Rosenthal, an avowed humanist who'd grown up speaking Yiddish in a religious Jewish home, was trying to understand the full weight of what it meant to Lowell to sully his family's reputation and undermine his straight white male, Protestant privilege by writing poetry in which he emasculated himself and revealed himself to be emotionally unstable, a lousy husband, a failed father, and a pretty unpleasant person. But the choice of the word "confession" to describe Lowell's poetry and of the phrase "soul's therapy" confusingly elides the Christian practice of confession with the secular practice of therapy and poetry.

The conflation of Christian practice and therapy results in a great many contradictions and confusions as to what "poetry as confession" is. When Rosenthal writes, "it is hard not to think of *Life Studies* as a series of personal confidences, rather shameful, that one is honor-bound not to reveal," what is the location of that shame? Is it in the nature of the secrets Lowell reveals or in his use of the poem as a public space for private material? Is it the shameful content of a poem or the expression of private content that makes a poem confessional? And, if it is the first, shameful according to whom? To God? To the state? To the mainstream culture? By this measure, any poem written in the United States in the 1950s or '60s that included homoerotic content could be considered confessional, but Allen Ginsberg is only sometimes considered confessional and Frank O'Hara almost never.

And what is the role of the reader? In "poetry as confession," is the reader a priest/analyst who offers absolution or provides a therapeutic context? Or is the reader a voyeur-witness intruding upon what should be a confidential exchange between poet and priest/analyst? These confusions matter. The poem in one case is a sign of health and in another a catalogue of sin. The poem is either a site of communication between poet and other or it is an intercepted, broken confidence.

One thing that confession and therapy have in common is that both require the presence of another human being. In this way, I find Rosenthal's metaphor to be apt and useful. Confessional poems are often addressed *to* someone—a priest, a therapist, a lover, a friend, a child, or the reader—in ways that break with traditional apostrophe in the lyric. In the lyric, apostrophe (the word comes from the Greek: "to turn away," meaning that the orator turns away to address an individual) is most often a trope of address to a dead, absent, or inanimate other or self. In his essay "Lyric, History, and Genre," Jonathan Culler writes:

> Apostrophe represents what is most embarrassing in lyric: the pretension to vatic action that critics prefer to evade, as they discuss instead, for instance, the theme of the power of poetic imagination . . .
>
> Apostrophe works to constitute a poetic speaker taking up an active relationship to a world or element of the world constructed as addressee.

It may be, then, that confessional poems employ apostrophe not in a way that breaks with the traditional lyric but in ways that foreground and emphasize what is "most embarrassing in lyric." Either way, the use of apostrophe is characteristic of confessional poems.

In a confessional, narrative poem, the poet often speaks to another specific, real person and thus breaks from the lyric notion that "eloquence is heard; poetry is overheard" (John Stuart Mill). Apostrophe is part of what gives confessional poetry a sense of "realness" and intimacy. Because apostrophe posits "an addressee which is often asked to respond in some way" (Culler again), it creates a sense of urgency in a poem as well as a sense of a vatic present. It's also part of what can position the reader as voyeur, because the reader is now in the position of witnessing two "real" people rather than listening to a person speaking to himself.

■ ■ ■

Wallace Stevens was interested in the imagination's ability to press "back against the pressure of reality." Anne Sexton's poems, which frequently employ direct address, often work to press her reality—her voice, will, physical (female) presence—against a male interlocutor who is limiting or suppressing her. The power of Sexton's poems comes as much or more from their direct address and the discomfort engendered by such an address as from her taboo, too-personal content, or I-ness.

In her long poem "The Double Image," Sexton addresses her daughter Joyce (four years old at the time). Sexton describes feeling intense guilt about being separated from Joyce. (These separations were caused by Sexton's suicide attempts and hospitalizations.) Sexton explores the tangled relationship between herself and Joyce and between Sexton and her own mother, with whom Sexton went to live, "like an angry guest, / like a partly mended thing, an outgrown child." Sexton reveals in "The Double Image" that her mother never forgave her for attempting suicide and accused Sexton of giving her cancer. In the poem, Sexton and her mother have their portraits painted. The portraits are hung on opposite walls, and Sexton describes her mother's portrait as "my mocking mirror, my overthrown / love, my first image."

The long poem ends with Sexton admitting:

> I didn't want a boy,
> only a girl, a small milky mouse
> of a girl, already loved, already loud in the house
> of herself. We named you Joy.
> I, who was never quite sure
> about being a girl, needed another
> life, another image to remind me.
> And this was my worst guilt; you could not cure
> nor soothe it. I made you to find me.

Personal confidences and private details abound in this poem, and the confession at the end—that Sexton made her daughter to find herself, to save herself—is a brave and horrible thing to say to a child and also a feeling that may be deeply common and true even if one is not suicidal or profoundly disturbed. The guilt, rage, jealousy, joy, love, pleasure of the cracked mirror of mother-daughterhood are taboo and archetypal.

Sexton wrote "The Double Image" while studying with John Holmes, her first workshop teacher. Holmes was dismayed and angry[5] when Sexton read him the poem and told her not to publish it. Sexton's poem "For John, Who Begs Me Not to Enquire Further" is her response to Holmes, who had characterized Sexton as a guilty, suicidal, deranged, excessive spectacle. In a letter to Maxine Kumin, Sexton's close friend, Holmes wrote: "She writes so absolutely selfishly, of herself, to bare and shock and confess. Her motives are wrong, artistically, and finally the self-preoccupation comes to be simply damn boring."

"For John, Who Begs Me Not to Enquire Further" is an apologia and ars poetica for Sexton's own poems and for confessional poetry more broadly, as well as a straightforward attempt to save face and, ultimately, save self and defend herself against Holmes's diminishing assessment of her. The title—itself a kind of apostrophe—refers to the epigraph of *To Bedlam and Part Way Back*, which is a quote from a letter in 1815 from Schopenhauer to Goethe:

It is the courage to make a clean breast of it in face of every question that makes the philosopher. He must be like Sophocles's Oedipus, who, seek-

5. I'm very interested in the relationship between anger and poetry. I'm interested when critics express anger in relation to a work of art or an artist. Anger is not the same as disappointment, dislike, or disapproval. I always wonder what is at stake for the critic in a particular work when the result is this kind of intense anger. Such anger is often justified, by the critic, as a natural result of feeling that the very art form is being threatened or that a person (the artist or the object of the artwork) is endangered by the work.

ing enlightenment concerning his terrible fate, pursues his indefatigable enquiry, even when he divines that appalling horror awaits him in the answer. But most of us carry in our heart the Jocasta who begs Oedipus for God's sake not to inquire further . . .

Confessional poetry is not just poetry that is personal. It is not just poetry about taboo subjects. Confessional poetry contains a quality of potential self-immolation that is best understood by imagining this moment when Oedipus asks Jocasta for the truth about his parentage. At this point, Jocasta knows that Oedipus, father of four of her children, is also her son. She knows that Oedipus accidentally fulfilled a prophecy, killed his father and married his mother (her), but she tries to put Oedipus off when he asks her who he is. In Sophocles's play, Jocasta says to Oedipus, "someone / who ignores all this bears life more easily . . . O you unhappy man! / May you never find out who you really are!"

As Schopenhauer knows, the philosopher has both Oedipus and Jocasta within, but the true philosopher continues to seek enlightenment no matter how horrible and despite the forces (our "defenses" in psychoanalytic terms) that beg our inner Oedipus to please, please stop asking. Sexton's title invokes the necessity for the poet of this potentially fatal quest for enlightenment. "For John, Who Begs Me Not to Enquire Further" begins:

> Not that it was beautiful,
> but that, in the end, there was
> a certain sense of order there;
> something worth learning
> in that narrow diary of my mind,
> in the commonplaces of the asylum
> where the cracked mirror

or my own selfish death
outstared me.

Sexton is saying to John Holmes (and others) that her commitment (compulsion?) to write about herself, including the "narrow diary of [her] mind" and "the commonplaces of the asylum," in a manner that Holmes characterized as selfish, shocking, boring, and overly preoccupied with herself, is the only way to approach "a certain order," an awareness (cracked, though it may be) of vision of truth and the truth of death. After all, death, madness, trauma, maternal and filial sorrow exist even if we choose not to look at them; they outstare us even if we stare at them.

Sexton continues:

> And if I tried
> to give you something else,
> something outside of myself,
> you would not know
> that the worst of anyone
> can be, finally,
> an accident of hope.
> I tapped my own head;
> it was glass, an inverted bowl.
> It is a small thing
> to rage in your own bowl.
> At first it was private.
> Then it was more than myself;
> it was you, or your house
> or your kitchen.
> And if you turn away

because there is no lesson here
I will hold my awkward bowl,
with all its cracked stars shining
like a complicated lie,
and fasten a new skin around it
as if I were dressing an orange
or a strange sun.
Not that it was beautiful,
but that I found some order there.
There ought to be something special
for someone
in this kind of hope.
This is something I would never find
in a lovelier place, my dear,
although your fear is anyone's fear,
like an invisible veil between us all . . .
and sometimes in private,
my kitchen, your kitchen,
my face, your face.

If Sexton only gives Holmes what he wants—"something outside of [her-self]"—it will not contain the things he needs to know, the things he is afraid to examine, because Holmes is afraid. (Holmes's fear is "anyone's fear," but, unlike Sexton, he is not able to overcome it.)

I love Sexton's lines, "It is a small thing / to rage in your own bowl," for the way she domesticates her own mind (or sees the way in which her mind is being domesticated by others) and turns her mind into the most primitive of (hu)man-made vessels. I love the way Sexton trans-forms or inverts the very word "small" into something complex, capacious, dangerous. It's not a pun, exactly, but a kind of inversion or autopsy of the word that reveals that the word's meaning depends on one's perspective, on whether one is inside or outside of the inverted bowl. Women are supposed to be small (in size). Small often means minor, inconsequential, or powerless. Small also means limited or parochial, as in "small-minded"—she has set us up for this reading with "that narrow diary of my mind" a few lines earlier. The John Holmeses of the world who expect poets, especially women poets, to write about something outside the self might imagine that it is a "small thing" (an easy thing) to rage in one's own bowl, to keep private what should be private, to stay in the house or kitchen, to seek out beauty and "a lovelier place," but it is *not* a small thing to Sexton. Nor is being trapped in an inverted bowl (or bell jar) a small thing. Sexton recognizes that the injunction to contain her rage, to not look at herself (too much), to write about something outside herself is an effort to make her small and keep her small and controllable. Sexton will not tolerate this misogynist stratagem.

Notice that Sexton does not say "rage in my own bowl." No, "it is a small thing to rage in *your* own bowl" [emphasis mine], writes Sexton. This is no careless slippage of pronouns. Sexton subtly, gently, smally acknowledges that she is not only trapped but *being trapped*, the "I" becomes "you," "my own head" becomes "an inverted bowl" becomes "your bowl," and what was, at first, "private" becomes "more than myself." If she is to rage in a bowl, it will be "more than [herself]," and if he turns away, she will shine "like a complicated lie" and "dress" her mind with new skin as if she were "an orange / or a strange sun." Here, Sexton uses a feminized verb, "dress," as her mind morphs from glass bowl to orange (the fruit) to sun, growing with each "small" transformation into something that is more life-giving and terrifying. You cannot find such "order" in a "lovelier place," Sexton explains. Poems that seek out such necessary and illuminating order (the sun!) will never be lovely places, and perhaps poets should also stop trying to be lovely. By the end of the poem the commas are splicing Holmes almost to death, splicing the "invisible veil between us all" (the veil is decorum, privacy, restraint, containment, the belittlement of women). Sexton cannot be contained. Sexton's kitchen is Holmes's kitchen, her face (fastened with a new skin) is Holmes's face. Does Holmes feel it is "a small thing" to rage inside an inverted, awkward bowl once he's in there with her (or instead of her)?

■ ■ ■

Whether it is the search for truth despite the potential horror that truth may bring or the shame of admitting one's sinfulness or the sin of breaking confidences, confessional poetry is marked by a sense of urgency and risk to the poet, to the people mentioned in the poem, and to the poem's readers.

> For the eyeing of my scars, there is a charge
> For the hearing of my heart——
> It really goes.
>
> And there is a charge, a very large charge,
> For a word or a touch
> Or a bit of blood

writes Sylvia Plath in "Lady Lazarus." By "charge," Plath means that there is both an excitement and a cost to the confessional poem, which often feels like the eyeing of the poet's scars. In the case of Plath's poems the scars often aren't scars yet; the wounds are too fresh. Reading Plath sometimes feels like watching someone cutting herself. The experience is horrifying, compelling, damaging, exciting, and dangerous.

Looking at these poems and poets, we must try to imagine what it meant to be writing in "the tranquilized *Fifties*," as Lowell called them—a time of intense repression when societal expectations about sex and gender were more rigid than they'd been since before the 1920s. We must try to imagine what it felt like in the late 1950s and early 1960s to admit that you'd had an abortion or to speak back to those who wished Sexton would *not* write the way she was writing, who wished she would not write at all. Confessional poetry, which may have begun as "soul's therapy"—talking about the self in order to create a more integrated self—was also a kind of public witnessing of a shared moment of cultural breakdown.

Lowell risked a lot when he wrote lines like, "I keep no rank nor station. / Cured, I am frizzled, stale and small" ("Home After Three Months Away") or, "my mind's not right" ("Skunk Hour") and

> I hear
> my ill-spirit sob in each blood cell,
> as if my hand were at its throat. . . .
> I myself am hell;
> nobody's here—

It was something unusual for someone like Lowell, who had ample rank and station, to admit to feeling that he had neither, to admit to being ill, frizzled, stale, small, and in hell. At the same time, it was his rank and station—his straight white male, *Mayflower* privilege—that may have enabled Lowell to risk this kind of writing. Certainly, it made his trespasses and self-revelations noteworthy. For example, when Rosenthal wrote his review of Lowell, he made no mention of Ginsberg's *Howl*, which was also about breakdown and which had violated social norms to such an extent that the book had provoked an obscenity trial.

It may have been easy for critics to dismiss Ginsberg's counterculture poetics as part and parcel of his status as a degenerate, homosexual Jew. John Hollander referred to *Howl* as a "dreadful little volume," and James Dickey wrote, "It takes more than this to make poetry." In "Poet of the New Violence," which appeared two years before his review of *Life Studies*, Rosenthal reviews *Howl and Other Poems* (which he refers to as "a pamphlet") with a mixture of disgruntled praise, disdain, and sympathy. Rosenthal calls Ginsberg's poems "striking" and acknowledges that this is "poetry of genuine suffering" and that "the agony, in any case, is real." But Rosenthal's assessment is mostly a convoluted, coded mess of less than subtle jabs. In the second paragraph, Rosenthal misgenders Ginsberg: "We have had smoking attacks on the civilization before, ironic or murderous or suicidal. We have *not* had this particular variety of anguished anathema-hurling in which the poet's revulsion is expressed with the single-minded frenzy of a raving madwoman." The following sentence, which took me many readings to parse, is a fascinating jumble of sarcasm and condescension:

> Ginsberg hurls, not only curses, but *everything*—his own paranoid memories of a confused, squalid, humiliating existence in the "underground" of American life and culture, mock political and sexual "confessions" (together with the childishly aggressive vocabulary of obscenity which in this country is being increasingly substituted for anti-Semitism as the "socialism of fools"), literary allusions and echoes, and the folk-idiom of impatience and disgust.

Rosenthal is accusing Ginsberg of being paranoid and confused and crit-
icizing Ginsberg for imagining that his homosexual-counterculture-
drug-using-Beatnik-"underground"-life is itself a literary achievement
or a form of effective political activism. Rosenthal's quotations around
"confessions" make it clear that he doesn't believe these are real confes-
sions or that Ginsberg's real confessions will be of much import. Gins-
berg's agony and suffering are real, as are the problems against which
Ginsberg "hurls" and "spews" his "false notes and postures," but Rosen-
thal is unconvinced of the literary merit of such a style and finds Gins-
berg's brand of extreme nonconformity misguided and dangerous.
Rosenthal does not want vulgarity or obscenity to be the new manifes-
tation of a "socialism of fools." In other words, vulgarity, unlike the "'ra-
tional discourse,' such as we find in almost all other American literature
of dissidence," is a form of "intellectual distortion" rather than an effi-
cacious mode of dissent and critique. Ultimately, Rosenthal, in a rather
homophobic and belittling way, dismisses Ginsberg literarily and polit-
ically: "This is all too destructive and therefore mistaken, and . . . a total
assault may be even worse than mere acquiescence."

No one denied that Ginsberg's work was radical, urgent, spectacular,
and disruptive. The question for the established or trying-to-be-estab-
lished literary critics was whether *Howl* was actually poetry, actually
worth reading, and whether this kind of "total assault" would either en-
ter the mainstream canon or change the canon and the establishment.
Rosenthal and other early reviewers treated Ginsberg as a sort of freak-
show spectacle and thought it likely Ginsberg would "screech himself
mute any moment now."

Lowell's personal breakdown was perceived very differently than

Ginsberg's or (soon afterwards) Plath's or Sexton's. I think this has largely to do with Lowell's status, despite his nervous breakdowns, as an insider—with his whiteness, straightness, Christianness, and pedigree. Ginsberg took drugs (and later used meditation and Buddhist practices) to expand his mind and free his creativity, to help him see beyond the horrible conformity and falsity of the establishment. Ginsberg was often singing, chanting prayers and mantras, handing out flowers, ringing bells, getting arrested. He talked openly about his sexuality, drug use, and counterculture views with pride, enthusiasm, and joy even to people like William F. Buckley Jr., even on television. By all accounts, Ginsberg was a loving son and sibling. From a young age, he was often in the position of having to care for his mother, Naomi, who was in and out of mental hospitals. Her mental illness affected Ginsberg deeply and terribly, but it was never kept secret within the family, which is partly why, I think, mental illness (while traumatic and full of grief) doesn't have the same overtones of shame as it does in the work of Lowell, Plath, and Sexton. Ginsberg seems to have had a warm and mutually loving relationship with his father, Louis Ginsberg, and they performed together as poets. Allen Ginsberg cared for his father until Louis died at the age of eighty, in 1976.

Lowell, on the other hand, took drugs—lithium finally gave Lowell some relief, but not entirely—to allow him to function in society. When he was manic, he could be cruel, out of control, and hurtful to those he loved. Lowell was frequently caught in a cycle of acting out and begging forgiveness. Lowell was a pacifist and spent several months in prison as a conscientious objector during World War II, but he was more often trying to fix himself, not upend the world around him. In this context, Lowell's individual break or breakdown become symbolic and emblematic of the larger problems and necessary shifts in society, whereas Ginsberg was an outsider, actively and passionately putting his queer shoulder to the wheel, hoping to break the whole machine of oppression, police brutality, mass incarceration, war, homophobia, sexual repression, and environmental destruction.

■　■　■

I will address the feminization of confessional poetry in a moment, but I hope it has not escaped anyone's notice that all the poets I've mentioned so far are white. For a long time I puzzled over the whiteness of confessional poetry and, to a lesser extent, the straightness. Why, I wondered, was Plath called confessional but not Gwendolyn Brooks? Why is Sharon Olds confessional but not Lucille Clifton? Why Lowell but not Frank O'Hara? When black poets write with I-ness about personal, private content, they are mostly called "black poets," if and when critics take their work seriously. When LGBTQ poets write urgent, silence = death, explicitly sexual, bodily poems, they are called "queer poets." The confessional label seems restricted to poets with mainstream privilege.

I once asked the poet Shane McCrae if he considered himself a confessional poet. He'd written that Plath was his earliest, most important influence, and I saw what I considered to be a strong confessional impulse in his work. McCrae responded (via email):

> I do think that it is in some ways impossible for a writer of color to *be* a confessional writer—or at least to be thought of as a confessional writer. Writers of color *absolutely* can write autobiographically. But I don't know that it is confessional. The *confessional* is the admitting of a step—or a fall— away from a state of grace. It is a report of grace momentarily destabilized.

But the assumption behind it is that grace is the default position. For writers of color, it is not assumed that grace is our default position—we are always tainted by the sin of being oppressed.

If confessionalism is built on the premise that only white people can fall from grace and that people of color are already "fallen," then the confessional designation is a white supremacist construction because it relies upon the notion that only white people occupy a state of grace from which to fall.

If confessional poetry came into being in part because of Lowell's whiteness, maleness, and straightness, how is it, then, that confessional poetry, in our day, is more strongly associated with Anne Sexton and Sylvia Plath (and with women in general) than with Lowell, John Berryman, or W. D. Snodgrass? How is it that confessional poetry became associated predominantly with (white) women? First of all, as I said before, I believe it was specifically Lowell's unique "fall from grace" that caused Rosenthal and others to view Lowell's shift in the last section of *Life Studies* as so culturally significant. Even though Sexton and Plath may have in fact influenced Lowell greatly while he was writing the final poems in *Life Studies* (remember that Lowell taught Sexton and Plath and read and commented on their work), their work was not published until after *Life Studies* (and in Plath's case, her fame and notoriety did not take hold until a decade later). Within a few years of Rosenthal's review, the poems of Sexton and Plath upstaged and outshone those of Lowell and other confessional male poets. Sexton and Plath, in large part because of the rise of the women's movement (or women's lib), garnered a passionate following among readers (predominantly women readers), which caused significant anxiety and disgust among critics.

Anne Sexton's first book, *To Bedlam and Part Way Back*, was published in 1960, just as the birth control pill was becoming available (initially only to married women). In 1963, Betty Friedan published *The Feminine Mystique*, Congress passed the Equal Pay Act, and 200,000 people gathered to hear Martin Luther King Jr. deliver his "I Have a Dream" speech. In 1964, Congress passed the Civil Rights Act, and there was a massive sit-in and protest in Berkeley. The National Organization for Women was founded in 1966, and, in 1968, women protested the Miss America Pageant, and the slogan "Sisterhood is powerful" was born. Soon after, "The personal is political" came into common usage as well.

In the introduction to *Poems from the Women's Movement*, Honor Moore writes:

> In 1966, when *Ariel* was published in the U.S., American women noticed. Not only women who ordinarily read poems, but housewives and mothers whose ambitions had awakened when they read Betty Friedan's *The Feminine Mystique* a few years earlier, and activists who came together to form the National Organization for Women (NOW) that same year. At the time, Plath was identified with the poets M. L. Rosenthal dubbed "confessional" . . . but that label obscured the significance of her posthumous volume. Here was one woman, superbly trained in her craft, whose final poems uncompromisingly charted her rage, ambivalence, and grief in a voice with which many women identified.

Within a few years, many of the things Rosenthal had noted in Lowell—intense, taboo-breaking poetry about the "predicament and horror of the lost Self," in which an unmasked poet brought private and personal concerns into the public realm—became a mode or style or volume of poetry that was associated with Plath and Sexton and with poets of the

65

women's movements. Although critics mostly did not deem poets like Audre Lorde, Adrienne Rich, Muriel Rukeyser, Sonia Sanchez, Denise Levertov, Maxine Kumin, Anne Waldman, Lucille Clifton, Diane di Prima, June Jordan, Carolyn Kizer, Marilyn Hacker, Toi Derricotte, and Molly Peacock confessional, what we now think of as confessional often comes from qualities we associate with the work of these poets.

This conflation of the confessional impulse with poetry by women, particularly women writing during the women's movements, occurred, in part, because of a very extreme reaction by the literary establishment to the immense popularity of Sexton and Plath during the late 1960s and early 1970s. Sylvia Plath's first book, *The Colossus*, was published in 1960 in England and two years later in the United States. It garnered a few positive and somewhat measured reviews. Plath's *Ariel* was published in England in 1965 and sold 15,000 copies within the first ten months. When Plath's novel, *The Bell Jar*, was published in the United States, in 1971, it was on the bestseller list for twenty-four weeks. Over the first two decades after its publication, *Ariel* sold more than half a million copies.

It is often posited that Plath's popularity was due to the mythology around her suicide (1963), but in her book *Sylvia Plath and the Mythology of Women Readers*, Janet Badia makes a powerful case for the fact that the rise in popularity of Plath's work did not occur, in earnest, for several years after Plath's death and that this popularity was largely due to the rise of the women's movements, particularly the creation of feminist magazines, newspapers, presses, and other feminist media outlets that sprang up in the late 1960s and '70s.

The idea that Plath's (and Sexton's) readership was garnered not because of the work's merits but because of readers' fascination with their suicidality and eventual deaths and because of readers' compulsion to (mistakenly) attribute a political (feminist) imperative to the work is part of what upset literary critics (even if they were often the ones perpetuating these ideas). The reviews of Plath and Sexton after they became popular are shockingly vitriolic and seem to be as much a criticism of the people who like Plath and Sexton as they are of Plath and Sexton's poems. "By the 1970s, if not earlier," writes Badia, "Plath's readers were perceived to be young (implicitly white) women who—in overprivileging the disturbed pathology ostensibly feeding the poetry—had 'misinterpreted' not only the tragedy of the situation but the work itself."

Badia performs a comprehensive examination of hundreds of reviews of Plath across five decades and convincingly makes the case that "anxieties about women readers have driven (indeed continue to drive) critical assessments of Plath's oeuvre, giving shape to everything from the language critics use when describing the work under review to the judgments they reach about its quality and literary worth." Badia notes that the criticism of Plath is similar in tone and content to the criticism of Kate Millett's *Sexual Politics* and writes, "I am suggesting that Plath's writing and its audience became such contested sites in large part because feminists were not the only ones with a vested interest in her writing during this time."

Here are a few excerpts of reviews of Plath, and Sexton, that I found (some in Badia and some in other books and essays):

In 1967, Al Alvarez, the poetry editor for *The Observer*, calls Plath "the patron saint of the feminists" and calls Plath readers "dissatisfied, family-hating shrews."

Helen Vendler, in *The Music of What Happens: Poems, Poets, Critics*, writes:

Sexton is most unlike Lowell. . . .

. . . The relentless centrality of the "I"—almost always indoors alone, contemplating its own anguish (even if sometimes in farcical terms)—is finally exasperating.

In Webster Schott's 1972 review of Plath's *Winter Trees*, he calls Plath "a sick woman who made art of her sickness. . . . Some young people, having limited experience, need literature to help them feel bad, and they will celebrate Plath for a while."

From Susan Wood's review in *Washington Post* "Book World":

Who will buy this book? I think, from hearing them speak at poetry readings and in poetry workshops, it is primarily young girls and women who admire Sexton for all the wrong reasons, making her a martyr to art and feminism; who seem, out of their own needs, to identify with her pathological self-loathing and to romanticize it into heroism. It has very little to do with poetry and it does neither poetry nor Anne Sexton a service.

"What emerges," writes Badia, "are anxieties, not only about the 'certain type of poetry' being published, but also about the kinds of readers and reading practices such publications invite." She explains:

To many of the critics writing at the time, especially to those schooled in either New Criticism or the high canonical modernist tradition of T. S. Eliot that sought to create a small, elite audience, Plath's work threatened to disrupt the very reputableness of the literary project and thus had to be contained. . . .

. . . Such anxieties mark the history of confessional poetry's reception and continue to shape how readers and critics regard those authors who, like Plath, have been and continue to be seen as confessional poets. An examination of this larger history shows that while the anxieties and ten-

sions that characterize the poetry's reception are complex—involving a tri-
angulation of more specific anxieties about genre, the subject matter of
poetry, and the perceived reader—they are often masked behind what ap-
pear to be purely aesthetic concerns.

From the beginning, the term "confessional" inspired concern. Concern
for Lowell's soul, for the feelings of those he exposed, for poets' mental
health, for the effect of this kind of poetry on its readers and on the genre
itself. This anxiety reached a fever pitch in response to the popularity of
Sexton and Plath and inspired a critical panic over what confessionalism
would do to poetry. This alarm can only be understood in the context
of the latent or blatant misogyny of male and female critics whose con-
demnation of the confessional (which by the mid-1970s had been con-
flated with the personal, the domestic, the direct, the strident, the daily,
the sexual, the narrative, the bodily, the outsider) serves to defend het-
eropatriarchy and maintain an elite (usually male) audience for poetry.

Concern about and for women readers is as old as the moment
women first learned to read and certainly predates the particular anxiety
about and for Plath and Sexton's readers. During the Victorian era,
medical authorities were concerned that women who engaged in "exces-
sive and unsupervised reading of popular fiction" would experience
"early menstruation, painful menses, and infertility, as well as nervous-
ness, insanity, and even premature death." Women poets and novelists
were outselling men when Nathaniel Hawthorne made his remark about
the "mob of scribbling women" who were ruining literature. The con-
cern for the "common" (i.e., female) reader, for the husbands of Plath's
readers ("dissatisfied, family-hating shrews"), for academia, for more se-
rious (male) writers, and for poetry—as if confessional poets were in-

fecting the genre with a terminal illness—takes hold at the same time that Plath and Sexton enter the scene.

I'm not saying that the critical response toward Plath and Sexton and toward their female readers is the only reason confessional poetry came to be associated with poetry by women. In her indispensable book of feminist literary and cultural criticism, *Stealing the Language: The Emergence of Women's Poetry in America*, Alicia Ostriker examines the role of the body, identity expression, anger and violence, female desire, the gendered nature of language, and the gendered nature of literary criticism as they relate to what she calls the "extraordinary tide of poetry by American women" writing in the 1960s and '70s. "We need to recognize," writes Ostriker, "that our customary literary language is systematically gendered in ways that influence what we approve and disapprove of, making it extremely difficult for us to acknowledge certain kinds of originality—of difference—in women poets." The aspects Ostriker explores are also at the heart of what defines a poem as confessional, including, of course, the poet's relationship to privacy.

The lyric was supposed to be a private, universal, impersonal, overheard address, but as Deborah Nelson points out in her book *Pursuing Privacy in Cold War America*, "privacy's deprivations belonged primarily to women and its autonomy to men." The breakdown of privacy by female and male writers in the 1960s had the effect of destabilizing the privilege of white heterosexual men for whom the lyric may have appeared to investigate "universal truths" when in fact the lyric ignored or devalued what Carolyn Kizer called "merely the private lives of one-half of humanity." The high value placed on decorum, modesty, and impersonality was a way of maintaining the status quo of straight white male plutocracy, which is part of why "The personal is political" became the rallying cry of second-wave feminism.

In her essay "My Name Is Darkness," Sandra Gilbert writes, "the self-defining confessional genre, with its persistent assertions of identity and its emphasis on a central mythology of the self, may be . . . a distinctively female poetic mode." Gilbert explains that the male poet may "manage to be 'at once private and public, lyrical and rhetorical' . . . because the personal crisis of the male poet 'is felt at the same time as a symbolic embodiment of national and cultural crisis.'" This ability to be simultaneously private and public, particular and universal, was not available to women, who had seen themselves and been seen only as muses and as the subjects of poems rather than the creators of selves and of art.

The primary characteristics of confessional poetry—private or personal content, reliance on lived experience, I-ness, direct address, urgency, and a sense of risk—were projected onto the poems from the women's movements, and confessional poetry began to be seen as any kind of poem (formal or free verse) that was personal, political, urgent, risky, accessible, and subversive. But to call the stylistically diverse poetry in which women speak truth to power despite enormous pressure "confessional" is to ignore the important fact that the poets of the women's movements were *not* confessing. Confession is the wrong word. These poets were *not* saying, "Bless me, Father, for I have sinned," and they were *not* asking for forgiveness. Listen:

> *I am not wrong: Wrong is not my name*
> My name is my own my own my own
> and I can't tell you who the hell set things up like this
> but I can tell you that from now on my resistance
> my simple and daily and nightly self-determination
> may very well cost you your life
>
> (JUNE JORDAN)

■ ■ ■

Whoever despises the clitoris despises the penis
Whoever despises the penis despises the cunt
Whoever despises the cunt despises the life of the child.
. . . .
Who will speak these days,
if not I,
if not you?

(MURIEL RUKEYSER)

■ ■ ■

and when we speak we are afraid
our words will not be heard
nor welcomed
but when we are silent
we are still afraid.

So it is better to speak
remembering
we were never meant to survive.

(AUDRE LORDE)

■ ■ ■

because a woman is acceptable if she is
weak
acceptable if she is a victim

acceptable also if she is an angry victim ("shrew," "witch")
a woman's sorrow is acceptable
a deodorized sanitized sterilized antiperspirant
grinning efficient woman is certainly acceptable

but who can tolerate the power of a woman
close to a child, riding our tides
into the sand dunes of the public spaces.

(ALICIA OSTRIKER)

■   ■   ■

come celebrate
with me that everyday
something has tried to kill me
and has failed.

(LUCILLE CLIFTON)

I draw your attention to the conflation of confessional poetry and the
women's movements for several reasons. First of all, it was the energy
and passion of the women's movements (and the civil rights movement,
the Black Power movement, the gay rights movement, the anti-Vietnam
War movement) that gave Sexton, Plath, Ginsberg, Amiri Baraka,
Gwendolyn Brooks, Adrienne Rich, and poetry itself a feeling of ur-
gency. What interest there is today in confessional poetry comes more
from its eventual connection with social activism, counterculture, and
protest than from a lasting concern for Robert Lowell's soul. Many po-
etry readers are drawn to activist energy, and poets and poetry readers

often seek out poetry because they feel marginalized, silenced, disenfranchised, or alienated.

The second reason it is important to scrutinize the connection between what was called confessional and poetry written by women is that this particularly gendered kind of negative assessment of confessional poetry (as Rosenthal might say) continues apace in our day.

From a 2010 review of Sharon Olds:

> Stylistically invariant since 1980, [Olds] writes about the female body in a deterministic, shamanistic, medieval manner. Infantilization packaged in pseudo-confession is her specialty. . . . Her poetry defines feminism turned upon itself, chewing up its own hot and bothered cadaver, exposed since the 1970s. Female poets in workshops around the country idolize her, collaborate in the masochism, because they say she freed them to talk about taboo subjects, she "empowered" them. . . . Has given confessionalism such a bad name it can't possibly recover.

Or the response of one reader on Goodreads, that my work "feels confessional in the worst sense of the word."

I think it is no coincidence that immediately following the emergence of the poetry of the women's movements, more abstract, theory-based practices like Language poetry and conceptual and avant-garde movements gained prominence at the same time that critics were wringing their hands over these scribbling or shrieking women. In questioning the nature of truth, sincerity, and authorship, Language poetry temporarily subsumed the "I." Poems were again spoken to the void, just when confessional poetry (misnomer that it was) and autobiographically transparent poetry by women and poets of color and queer writers became popular.

Beginning in the '80s and '90s, poets who wanted to be taken seriously but also wanted to include narrative and emotional content used "elliptical" strategies to tell the truth but tell it slant. "Elliptical" is a term coined by Steph Burt in a review of Susan Wheeler's *Smokes* to describe the way some poets "try to manifest a person—who speaks the poem and reflects the poet—while using all the verbal gizmos developed over the last few decades to undermine the coherence of speaking selves." Although the work of many so-called elliptical poets had real political force and power behind it, the trickle-down effect was that MFA students and others studying and reading this work began to use "I" in a low- or no-stakes way. Many of the poems of this era were accessible and transparent like confessional poetry and had the narrative chattiness of New York School poems, but these poems were so allergic to sincerity and sentimentality that they hardly ever strayed from an apolitical, apathetic, flat-affect style. David Trinidad calls these kinds of poems "twists and turns of nothing." They are poems addressed to no one and about no one in which nothing is at stake.

Many of the things that compelled Lowell, Sexton, and Plath—mental illness, surveillance, police brutality, war, family, violence—have followed us into the twenty-first century, and the poets I care about are still writing about these problems. The poets I care about are writing about the systematic, institutional violence against people of color, LGBTQIA people, undocumented immigrants, poor people, and differently abled people. The poets I care about are writing about the prison industrial complex, the violence of borders, and the destruction of the environment.

Who decides what one can or should write about? Who gets to write from the "I"? Who has the right to speak? How can "I" name theirselves/ourselves/myself as specifically and honestly as possible in a way that does not depend upon creating a "you" that is othered in racist, homophobic, sexist, xenophobic, Islamophobic, or otherwise oppressive ways?

The question of who gets to say what and in what way is central to many poets writing today. Issues around permission and who gets called what—as well as how one is perceived if one writes out of lived experience or not—underlie our conversations about what poems should look and sound like, what poems are for, who poems are for, and the relationship between poetry, identity, and politics. This is our most urgent American conversation.

Over the years, students have asked me, "Can I write about my ex-boyfriend?" or, "Can I write about being from the South?" "Can I write about my difficult feelings about my mother, my brother, sex, coming out, depression, blackness, my Asian ancestry, my father's death, gun violence, race, the Middle Passage, rape?" Students ask if they can write about things that have or have not happened to them, that for one reason or another they are afraid to write about. "Of course," I always say. Students bring me these poems and hold them out in a shaky hand. They often say, "I've never written about this before," or, "I'm not sure this is even a poem."

Students come to me because I've written about the things that scare me most, and I have asked them to do the same. I've written about myself and my family, my body, my feelings in overtly autobiographical ways. Until recently, this had not been very difficult for me. As a Jew, I was taught that only actions can be sinful, never thoughts, and I come from a long line of truth-telling wordsmiths and provocateurs: Lenny Bruce, Allen Ginsberg, Woody Allen, Philip Roth, Bob Dylan, Sacha Baron Cohen. Art was always associated, for me, with "shock" rather than comfort, and I always felt it was more important to say what needed to be said than to make something beautiful. For a long time, being called confessional did not offend me. I did not at first understand the extent to which being called confessional depends upon my white privilege and I did not mind being called a woman poet or even a "mommy" poet, because I'm comfortable with the way my poetry arises from my female experience.

At the same time, there is pressure to write confessionally because this is the kind of writing that brought many of us to poetry, and we know how pleasurable it can be for our audiences. Some of us want to write for (and to) a less rarified audience, and transparent, autobiographical, socially oriented poetry appeals to a general audience. On the other hand, there is pressure to eschew directness and narrativity, to explore or embrace the kind of difficulty, indirection, and universality, we've been taught distinguishes serious poetry from populist writing.

It is a mistake to think that M. L. Rosenthal's "Poetry as Confession" review discerned or created a school or movement, but I do think Rosenthal astutely noticed a *moment* in the history of poetry in the United States in which poets started to sound different, started to use poems differently, and started to want something different from poems. But what if, instead of spotlighting the publication of *Life Studies* as this pivotal moment, Rosenthal had attributed this shift to *Howl*? After all, Michael McClure, present at the Six Gallery when Ginsberg read "Howl" aloud for the first time, described it like this: "Ginsberg read on to the end of the poem, which left us standing in wonder, or cheering and wondering, but knowing at the deepest level that a barrier had been broken, that a human voice and body had been hurled against the harsh wall of America."

Or what if, instead of testifying at the obscenity trial as to whether or not *Howl* was literature or not, whether it was obscene or not, whether it was original or not, all the big-deal professors spent their time writing and talking about the influence of jazz on *Howl* or the work and influence of Bob Kaufman? What if Kaufman's *Abomunist Manifesto* had become more popular than *Howl*, and Kaufman had been the most famous Beat poet instead of taking a vow of silence of ten years? What if the pivotal moment had come before the end of the 1950s? What if Langston Hughes's poem "Let America Be America," written in 1935, had been taken up as a rallying cry by all the people who felt "America was never America to me"—black people, Native people, immigrants, poor white people (just to name those mentioned in Hughes's poem)—and what if the swell of that poem's power had made the 1950s less "tranquilized"? Or what if, in 1958, after Hughes recorded his poems with Charles Mingus on the album *Weary Blues*, no one ever wanted to hear poetry *without* music again?

In 1949, Ginsberg spent eight months in a psychiatric hospital but did not receive treatment. With the help of two Columbia professors—Mark Van Doren and Lionel Trilling—Ginsberg had used the insanity plea as a way of avoiding jail time when he was arrested as an accomplice to robbery because he was caught in a stolen car and was discovered to have stolen goods in his apartment. (He hadn't stolen the goods or the car.) Etheridge Knight, a black poet who had served in Korea for three years and returned home traumatized, wounded, and addicted to opiates, was offered no insanity plea when he was arrested for armed robbery in 1960. Ginsberg openly advocated the use of LSD and marijuana (and used both himself), and although he was hassled by the police and arrested several times for protesting, he was never incarcerated. In the eight years that Knight spent in prison, Ginsberg became famous. While Knight was in prison, Ginsberg and his life-partner, Peter Orlovsky, lived off the royalties of *Howl* and off of Orlovsky's disability checks that he received for his service in the Korean War.

In the 1960s, Lowell's breakdown was seen, by the literary establishment, as emblematic of America's breakdown. Ginsberg's breaking away was seen as naive, annoying, fringe, subculture nonsense. Langston Hughes's shorter, less threatening poems were given a few pages in otherwise all-white anthologies. Bob Kaufman took a vow of silence in 1963, and Etheridge Knight was in prison. Despite winning the Pulitzer Prize in 1950 for *Annie Allen*, Gwendolyn Brooks was not seen by literary critics as a figure who would disrupt their lives or American poetry. I think this was because Brooks wrote about life on the street, which was as foreign to white, male critics as someone writing from another country. In the late '60s and early '70s Plath and Sexton's popularity was chalked up as evidence of the poor reading taste of hysterical girls and strident feminists. The rising tide of poets of the women's movements were dismissed as political and unliterary.

The "what if" game gets increasingly awful and harrowing the farther we stray from the privileges and protections that kept someone as ill as Lowell able to survive and often thrive, able to keep writing, keep being published, widely read, discussed, appreciated, and able to change the course of American poetry. Without money, whiteness, maleness, straightness, educational privilege, without the wives and close literary friends who were able to care for Lowell and for his legacy, such a breakdown would not have been seen as representational or deeply significant. Most poets who strayed from the mainstream because of who they were or because of their radical use of form or inclusion of previously taboo content were neither seen nor heard—these voices were often silenced by incarceration, illness, poverty, and violence.

I don't know what word Rosenthal would have used to describe Ginsberg's barrier-breaking poem had he not been too afraid of and overwhelmed by it to do more than mock and condescend. If Rosenthal had asked me (even though I wasn't born yet), I would have suggested "disobedience," though Alice Notley hadn't yet written "The Poetics of Disobedience." Ginsberg brought taboo, personal, sexual content into the public realm. Ginsberg was unmistakably, unequivocally, irrepressibly himself in his poems. His poems are spoken to real people, to God, to the state, to me, and though, at times, they are deranged, they are not ashamed. They do not seek forgiveness.

I don't know if poetry or the world would have been any different if I were now writing about a movement or a moment called "disobedience poetry" rather than "confessional poetry," but in my fantasy, Allen Ginsberg, Etheridge Knight, Gwendolyn Brooks, Audre Lorde, Alice Notley, C. D. Wright, Bernadette Mayer, Claudia Rankine, D. A. Powell, Brenda Hillman, Sharon Olds, June Jordan, Adrienne Rich, Alicia Ostriker, Sonia Sanchez, Eileen Myles, Langston Hughes, Morgan Parker, Danez Smith, Arielle Greenberg, Olena Kalytiak Davis, Ronaldo Wilson, Anne Waldman, Molly Peacock, Shane McCrae, Ross Gay, and so many others are all in it. No one wastes time accusing these poets of narcissism, hysteria, directness, accessibility, or for being strident or difficult, because their poems run on the engine of risk, which is different from the engine of shame.

In her book *End of the Sentimental Journey*, Sarah Vap writes, "I am against being against the sentimental." This helps me. I cannot say that I am for the confessional. What I can say is that I am against being against the confessional.

To be against the confessional is to be against writing about women and women's bodies, people of color and the bodies of people of color, queerness, trans bodies, differently abled bodies, individuality, oppression, perversity, diversity, class, the domestic, the non-normative, the personal, the political, the specific, the urgent, the spiritual, the banal, the direct, the relational, the screamed, the whispered. To be against the confessional is to be against coming out, against emphatically bringing the unwanted and repressed and hated and oppressed into the public view, into the poem.

"Poetry," wrote Audre Lorde, "is the way we help give name to the nameless so it can be thought."

Alice Notley wrote: "Staying alert to all the ways one is coerced into denying experience, sense and reason is a huge task."

I am not advocating any one kind of poetry. I want neither a prohibition of lived experience nor a tyranny of lived experience. I want poetry to lead us into less binary ways of thinking and living and writing and reading. I want a poetry that is catholic only in its lowercase sense: diverse, inclusive, and all-embracing.

A VERY LARGE CHARGE

THE ETHICS OF "SAY EVERYTHING" POETRY

A few years ago, John Murillo delivered a craft talk at Adelphi University, titled "Family Business: Elegy and the Ethics of Confession," in which he talks about three kinds of poems—elegies, poems of witness, and confessional-narrative poems. These three different modes all raise the question: "Do we have the right to use the lives of others as fodder?"

To explore this question, Murillo compares Kant's notion of the categorical imperative, in which Kant says that one should only act the way one thinks all people should act, to Jeremy Bentham's philosophy of utilitarianism, which asserts that a person should act in a way that creates the most happiness. Murillo talks about how his own work's purpose is to write "things I've seen, done, and heard about and . . . tell the stories others can't tell." Murillo asks: "You have a right to your own story . . . but you're also a member of a community. . . . To whom do you owe allegiance? Your family, the poem?"

Murillo explains that when writing a poetry of witness, a poetry in which one speaks for someone who supposedly cannot, one necessarily runs the risk of violating someone else's privacy and/or appropriating or exploiting another person's story and experience for one's own purposes. From a Kantian perspective, this is unethical. In a Kantian framework, the ends do *not* justify the means: one should not engage in a kind of writing that hurts or uses others. Murillo says: "All this [writing about other people] is immoral—we are using people, their history . . . the end can be the art itself or what can be gained from the art (fame, prizes, etc.)." But Murillo also says, later in the talk, "Even when I'm appropriating or exploiting, I can do it in a way that will bring some happiness." Writing a poem about or for someone who cannot write or speak (either literally or, more often, metaphorically) may benefit others, which—from a utilitarian point of view—creates happiness and is, therefore, ethical.

In the end, Murillo's answer to the question of whether the artist has the right to use other people's lives as creative fodder is this: "It's unethical, but it's what we do. . . . Ours is a dirty business. . . . What's the alternative?" I respect the uneasy, contradictory place Murillo comes to, the way he doesn't let himself off the hook. He knows he's wrong by at least one ethical measurement and he knows that being wrong has consequences. He's not going to stop thinking about ethics, but he's also not going to stop writing. I love Murillo's poems! I'm glad he won't stop writing them.

And what would poetry be if people only wrote "harmless" poems? Should we invent a litmus test to measure hurtfulness and put a "no one was harmed in the making of these poems" sticker on qualifying books? When I imagine a kind of poetry that tries not to hurt anyone I can only imagine a poetry so obscure, coy, abstract as to be unintelligible. I can't think of a poem (or book of poems) I love that would qualify. Still, I want to try to push past "it's wrong but it's what we do." If it's really wrong, perhaps we should not do it.

■　■　■

Sharon Olds's poem "I Go Back to May 1937" was originally published in 1987 in her book *The Gold Cell*. Olds used the last few lines of this poem as an epigraph to her 2004 selected collection, the title of which—*Strike Sparks*—also comes from this poem, which suggests that for Olds this poem offers a sort of retrospective ars poetica:

I GO BACK TO MAY 1937

I see them standing at the formal gates of their colleges,
I see my father strolling out
under the ochre sandstone arch, the
red tiles glinting like bent
plates of blood behind his head, I
see my mother with a few light books at her hip
standing at the pillar made of tiny bricks,
the wrought-iron gate still open behind her, its
sword-tips aglow in the May air,
they are about to graduate, they are about to get married,
they are kids, they are dumb, all they know is they are
innocent, they would never hurt anybody.
I want to go up to them and say Stop,
don't do it—she's the wrong woman,
he's the wrong man, you are going to do things
you cannot imagine you would ever do,
you are going to do bad things to children,
you are going to suffer in ways you have not heard of,
you are going to want to die. I want to go
up to them there in the late May sunlight and say it,
her hungry pretty face turning to me,
her pitiful beautiful untouched body,

his arrogant handsome face turning to me,
his pitiful beautiful untouched body,
but I don't do it. I want to live. I
take them up like the male and female
paper dolls and bang them together
at the hips, like chips of flint, as if to
strike sparks from them, I say
Do what you are going to do, and I will tell about it.

This is a poem of witness: Olds chooses to speak for her own preconception, preverbal self, for her child self, and for children and adults who have had bad things done to them. It's a confessional poem and a kind of elegy. The poem defines the role of the poet as truth-teller, a connection that comes up over and over in Olds's work and, of course, predates Olds and goes back further than I can trace.

Many people—myself included—admire Olds's fearlessness and explicitness and identify with her subject matter and with her insistence on speaking her truth. However, Olds's work has also garnered negative responses. Some criticize her work for being "stylistically invariant" or for the same things people love most about her work—that the poems are explicit about female experience, especially desire, motherhood, and the cisgender female body, and that they mix violence and sexuality.

Like many so-called confessional poets, Olds's poet-speaker seems to be hurting herself more than others, but many of Olds's poems have the potential to hurt her parents, her children, her spouse, and perhaps friends as well as herself. Perhaps in "I Go Back to May 1937" our concern is mollified because this poem occupies an imaginative space. We know Olds cannot actually go back to the time before her own birth and change anything. When she says, "I don't do it" (meaning, she doesn't stop her parents from getting married), we know that, in fact, she *cannot* stop them. When Olds says, "I want to live," this is a literary embrace of life, not a literal, anti-suicidal stance. But this poem still raises important ethical questions, including, "Is it OK to use other people's lives as fodder?"

Olds's poetry, which she calls "apparently very personal," sometimes feels more documentary than confessional and often raises some of the same ethical problems raised by photography. I want the photographer to take the photograph, especially when this "evidence" is all one has. Documentary photography is both necessary and ethical from a utilitarian perspective. Bringing images from the front to civilians has changed public opinion, ended wars, exposed wrongdoing. We want—we need—the photographer to "tell about it." But sometimes, especially with the most disturbing and urgent of photographs, we want the photographer to throw the about-to-be-shot victim to the ground, put a blanket around the naked child, scream "STOP!" Do something, anything—screw the photograph!

Poetry isn't journalism. I'm not saying Olds is reporting from the front, but I am saying that the stakes are high and that Olds's poems have changed if not saved lives. In the title poem, which is also the first poem of Olds's first book, *Satan Says*, published in 1980, the speaker-poet imagines herself trapped in a box. The only way out is to say what Satan wants her to say.

> I am trying to write my
> way out of the closed box
> redolent of cedar. Satan
> comes to me in the locked box
> and says, *I'll get you out. Say*

My father is a shit. I say
my father is a shit and Satan
laughs and says, *It's opening.*
Say your mother is a pimp.
My mother is a pimp. Something
opens and breaks when I say that.
My spine uncurls in the cedar box
like the pink back of the ballerina pin
with a ruby eye, resting beside me on
satin in the cedar box.
Say shit, say death, say fuck the father,
Satan says, down my ear.
The pain of the locked past buzzes
in the child's box on her bureau, under
the terrible round pond eye
etched around with roses, where
self-loathing gazed at sorrow.
Shit. Death. Fuck the father.
Something opens. Satan says
Don't you feel a lot better?
Light seems to break on the delicate
edelweiss pin, carved in two
colors of wood. I love him too,
you know, I say to Satan dark
in the locked box. I love them but
I'm trying to say what happened to us
in the lost past.

In this poem, Olds says what Satan wants her to say. She says, perhaps,
what *she* wants or needs to say because she is trying to say what happened

in the lost past. Again, she is witnessing for herself—and for children, more broadly—in spite of enormous pressure not to speak of family trauma and abuse.

From this "first poem" to her 2012 book, *Stag's Leap*, the cost of writing, to the self and to others, is high. In the title poem of *Stag's Leap*, Olds writes:

> And when I wrote about him, did he
> feel he had to walk around
> carrying my books on his head like a stack of
> posture volumes, or the rack of horns
> hung where a hunter washes the venison
> down with the sauvignon?

Olds is describing the breakup of her long marriage. The speaker's husband leaves her for another woman, and this, according to Olds's "apparently very personal" book of poems, is the primary reason for the breakup. But there are several hints that Olds's role as a writer, specifically as the writer of their family life, was complicated for her husband and perhaps caused instability in the marriage. In "Stag's Leap," the husband must manage the speaker's books—"a stack of / posture volumes"—that quickly become the rack of horns. Suddenly, the books-as-rack-of-horns are all that remain of the husband, who is dehumanized, made into a stag, and almost immediately disembodied, all in a few lines. The rack of horns is a symbol of cuckoldry. The husband is cuckolded by the poet even though the speaker is the one cuckolded by the husband's affair. The implication is that the threat or existence of the speaker's books (which I read not only as the finished book-objects but also as the act of writing about him and the family) cause the husband to have to stand up straighter, to comport himself with caution and care. But caution is not enough; the speaker, through her writing, becomes the hunter and washes down the killed, cooked husband with a glass of sauvignon.

■ ■ ■

Robert Lowell's 1973 book *The Dolphin* also portrays the end of a marriage; in this case, the end of Lowell's marriage to Elizabeth Hardwick (his second wife and mother of their daughter, Harriet). In 1970, Lowell left Hardwick for Lady Caroline Blackwood (whom Lowell nicknamed "Dolphin"). All three of the books Lowell published in 1973—*History*, *For Lizzie and Harriet*, and *The Dolphin*—contain poems about (and mention by name) Hardwick, Blackwood, Harriet Lowell, Sheridan Lowell (his son with Blackwood), Ivana (Blackwood's daughter), and other family and friends. Lowell's poem "To Speak of the Woe That Is in Marriage" is contained entirely within quotation marks and appears to be the wife's version of the poem "Man and Wife," which immediately precedes it in the last section of *Life Studies*. Perhaps this is Lowell's attempt to allow the figure of the wife a voice or agency; at the same time, "To Speak of the Woe That Is in Marriage"—a fourteen-line poem in rhymed couplets with regular meter—does not pretend to be regular speech, and is, therefore, clearly the constructed language of the poet speaking through the figure of the wife. *The Dolphin*, on the other hand, contains mostly unrhymed sonnets of irregular meter, several of which are meant to be in the voices of Harriet and Hardwick and several of which contain actual words and phrases from Hardwick's personal letters.

In "Dolphin," the title poem and the last poem in the book, Lowell is aware of the potential harm such appropriation and exposure might cause. The last eight lines of this final, fifteen-line sonnet are:

> I have sat and listened to too many
> words of the collaborating muse,
> and plotted perhaps too freely with my life,
> not avoiding injury to others,
> not avoiding injury to myself—
> to ask compassion . . . this book, half fiction,
> an eelnet made by man for the eel fighting—
>
> my eyes have seen what my hand did.

The Dolphin won the Pulitzer Prize in 1974, despite the fact that all three of Lowell's 1973 books were generally poorly reviewed and garnered several strong personal criticisms from Lowell's close friends and contemporaries. Lowell's friend Elizabeth Bishop wrote to Lowell (before publication of *The Dolphin*):

> I'm sure my point is only too plain . . . Lizzie is not dead, etc.—but there is a "mixture of fact & fiction," and you have *changed* her letters. That is "infinite mischief," I think. The first one, page 10, is so shocking—well, I don't know what to say. And page 47 . . . and a few after that. One can use one's life as material—one does, anyway—but these letters—aren't you violating a trust? IF you were given permission—IF you hadn't changed them . . . etc. But *art just isn't worth that much*. I keep remembering Hopkins' marvelous letter to Bridges about the idea of a "gentleman" being the

highest thing ever conceived—higher than a "Christian" even, certainly than a poet. It is not being "gentle" to use personal, tragic, anguished letters that way—it's cruel.[1]

Michelle Dean posits, in her 2016 *New Republic* review of Jeffrey Meyers's book *Robert Lowell in Love*,[2] that while Lowell slightly altered some of these poems after Bishop's criticism and while the line "my eyes have seen what my hand did" may indicate Lowell's surfacing conscience, Lowell's remorse was limited, at best. Dean writes:

> It is clear that Lowell had "seen" the damage he'd done to Hardwick's life, and to his daughter's. He may, at certain points, have been self-critical about it. But at the time he actually published *The Dolphin* he did not seem to feel particularly bad about it. To Bishop, he replied that he didn't think using the letters was slanderous, and that his use of Hardwick's actual words was "the poignance of the book, tho that hardly makes it kinder to her." Lowell continued, "It's oddly enough a technical problem as well as a gentleman's problem." His remorse, as performed in the poem, can't quite negate the coolness with which he decided to go forward, anyway. He had decided, despite Bishop's warning, that *art was worth that much.*

Adrienne Rich's 1973 review of *The Dolphin*, published in the *American Poetry Review*, is even more pointedly (and publicly) critical. Rich writes:

> What does one say about a poet who, having left his wife and daughter for another marriage, then titles a book with their names, and goes on to ap-

1. www.theparisreview.org/blog/2017/02/08/infinite-mischief
2. www.newrepublic.com/article/128999/robert-lowells-tainted-love

propriate his ex-wife's letters written under the stress and pain of deser-
tion, into a book of poems nominally addressed to the new wife? . . .

. . . I think this is bullshit eloquence, a poor excuse for a cruel and shal-
low book.

Rich's assessment of Lowell's work as "bullshit eloquence," and harsh
things that Lowell subsequently said about Rich and her work, led to the
end of their friendship. As Bishop suspected, Lowell did not stop the
publication of *The Dolphin*. Nor was he changed or chastened by Rich's
assessment. Apparently, relying on one's friends as moral compass—
even if one has friends as literarily brilliant and thoughtful as Bishop and
Rich—is not a foolproof way to figure out what to write and publish eth-
ically.

■ ■ ■

In "The Easel," also in *Stag's Leap*, Olds wonders, more directly than in
"Stag's Leap," about the effect of her writing (both the content of her
art and her ambition to be an artist) on her marriage/family:

> What if someone had told me, thirty
> years ago: If you give up, now,
> wanting to be an artist, he might
> love you all your life—what would I
> have said? I didn't even have an art,
> it would come from out of our family's life—
> what could I have said: nothing will stop me.

My work has come, like Olds's, from out of my "family's life." I've
pushed the limits of propriety and privacy in my work, run the risk of

embarrassing myself by disclosing too much or of harming my husband and children with my poems. Olds's poems—as well as the poems and the legacy of what I'm calling "the confessional impulse"—gave me the courage (the mandate? the permission?) to write about the female body, *my* female body, including birth, miscarriage, child rearing, and depression, to use "I" in my poems, to use an "I" that is apparently me, Rachel Zucker—to write, for example, poems about birthing, nursing, maternal ambivalence, a long marriage, restlessness, sex, lack of sex, desire, aging, and disappointment. Writing these poems clearly has personal value: writing these poems helps me understand and contextualize my experiences, which is healing for me and for others. But to write these poems out of my family's life—what else would I write about?—is to use my family (and other real people) as fodder, as "low-quality feed we give to domesticated animals" or "a thing or person regarded only for a specific use." Of course it is *not* alright to use people as fodder, and in the aftermath of my mother's death, I began to feel that something *should* stop me. I began to wonder what could, what would?

I find Olds's work permission-giving, risky, glorious, and enduring. I find Lowell's work, save for a few truly heartbreakingly moving poems, to be mostly "bullshit eloquence" and "not worth" the harm they caused. What does this mean about my own transgressions? As Lowell wrote, "my eyes have seen what my hand did." How can I, by reading the work of these recent masters, determine the nature of what my hand did? How can I forge a path forward? Is there any path forward that does not involve great, unforgivable harm?

Olds has talked, in interviews, about overcoming her fear of and belief in hell, a product of her Episcopalian childhood. I've had less to overcome in this way, having never been brought up to believe in hell, heaven, original sin, penance, or even that one's thoughts and feelings could qualify as sins. I was never concerned for my soul or for anyone's soul, only for the feelings and well-being of real people—even, I suppose, dead people. From a Jewish perspective, many of Olds's poems violate the commandment "Honor thy father and mother," and many confessional poems commit *lashon hara*, speaking ill of (or bad-mouthing) someone, which is considered a grave misdeed.

According to Jewish law, however, one *is* allowed to break any commandment, including *lashon hara*, in order to save a life. I do feel that Olds is often writing to save her own life and has saved and enriched the lives of so many others with her poems. I believe poems have social value. Muriel Rukeyser wrote, "What would happen if one woman told the truth about her life? / The world would split open." The world hasn't split open, but several people have come to me in tears, thanking me for my poems. My intuition tells me that these poems are ethical, but based on what?

Perhaps Olds's parents and ex-husband deserve the poems written about them, but what about her children? Years ago, Olds removed her children's names from subsequent printings of her books, but they are still identifiable as her children. Olds refuses, consistently, to discuss her personal life in interviews. When a Salon.com interviewer asked her, "Do you ever wonder what one of your children will think when he or she reads one of your poems that might be, at least in some small way, about them?" Olds replied:

> It's a wonderful question, and it's not one I can answer, really. Ten years ago I made a vow not to talk about my life. Obviously, the apparently very personal nature of my writing made this seem to me like maybe a good idea, for both sides of the equation—both for the muses and for the writer.

But it's a wonderful and important question. I think the thing that's most important to me about it is this idea that every writer has to decide these things for themselves, and we learn by making mistakes. We learn by finding out, five years later, what we wish we hadn't done. I've worked out this thing I've called "the spectrum of loyalty and betrayal." Which is also the spectrum of silence and song. And at either end, we're in a dangerous state, either to the self, or to others. We all try to fall in the right place in the middle.

Olds's poems, no matter what she does or does not reveal in interviews, rely, in part, on the excitement and discomfort of being led to believe that she is speaking the truth and speaking about lived experience and about real people. Olds's poems would not have the same "charge" without their sense of realness and of trespass. By "charge" I am referring to the lines from Sylvia Plath's poem "Lady Lazarus": "For the eyeing of my scars, there is a charge / For the hearing of my heart—— / It really goes. // And there is a charge, a very large charge / For a word or a touch / Or a bit of blood."

Once, the poet Craig Morgan Teicher said to me that the "charge" of my poetry for him partly lay in wondering what my husband thought about my poems. Many readers have asked me about this. Frankly, my husband is a bit of an exhibitionist and likes to be written about. For now, at least, he assures me that my poems do not rest heavy on his head like a stack of posture volumes, that the poems do not cuckold or dehumanize, debase or objectify him. He seems to feel that, by writing about him and putting these poems into the public realm, I'm committing an act of love and intimacy, attention and interest. My husband's feelings might change. If they do, we're screwed. And, in any case, his approval is not the end of the story of what is or is not ethical.

In her book *The Red Parts*, Maggie Nelson describes sending her mother the manuscript of *Jane*, a book Nelson wrote about her aunt Jane, who was murdered before Nelson was born.

> I sent galleys of *Jane* to my mother for her sixtieth birthday. I was nervous; I knew the book would immerse her in the details of a story she'd been trying to put behind her for thirty-five years. More than nervous—I was terrified. As I addressed the package to her in California, it occurred to me that the book might not constitute a gift at all. If she hated it, it could be construed as a birthday-ruining disaster, a bomb, a betrayal.
>
> I was hugely relieved when she called me after finishing the manuscript. She was in tears, saying she would be eternally grateful both to it and to me. She said it was a miracle: even though I never knew Jane, somehow I had managed to bring her back to life.

Did I imagine that my mother would respond similarly to the manuscript of *MOTHERs*? Perhaps I did. Perhaps I hoped that she would see that writing was my way of paying close attention to her and to our relationship and that close attention was an act of love. But, of course, such attention can also be an act of retribution, damage, appropriation, and violence.

For years, when my students asked me if it was alright to write about their parents, their lovers, themselves, their bodies, I told them, Yes, yes, you must. Now I am not always sure what to say. I love that Olds's "spectrum of loyalty and betrayal" is a spectrum and not a binary, but I'm uncomfortable with the notion that loyalty equals silence and that all song is a betrayal of sorts. So, how do I occupy an ethical position between silence and song?

■ ■ ■

This is not just an issue for confessional poets. It is, in a way, a problem that concerns all poetry written about real people. Journalists have codes of ethics, as do physicians, but poets do not. Is that because poetry does not seem, like medicine, a matter of life and death? Or because, unlike journalism, it seems like a hobby rather than a profession? Or because poetry exists almost entirely outside the market, and, therefore, even a poet who "exploits" others is not likely to gain financially? Or do poets lack a code of ethics because American poetry is so marginalized that we are not so worried about violating anyone's privacy with so few readers?

None of these is an ethical defense. The poet Saeed Jones tweeted, "You know . . . it's WILD how many poets get a pass on the blatant racism / misogyny in their work because of poetry's relative obscurity." Jones's tweet, on March 15, 2015, was in response to a reading at Brown University, two days earlier, in which conceptual poet Kenneth Goldsmith "remixed"—which is to say, slightly reordered—the autopsy report of Michael Brown, a black man killed by the police, and read this piece, which he called "The Body of Michael Brown." Goldsmith's performance engendered hurt and angry responses that decried Goldsmith as racist, exploitative, and insensitive for consciously or unconsciously reifying, perpetuating, and replicating the racist stereotypes he supposedly intended to criticize or subvert. The reactions that resulted—especially the deeply disturbing, mostly online defense of Goldsmith by some white, male poets who cry "censorship" when anyone criticizes Goldsmith or conceptual poets like Goldsmith—signal the need for a conversation that should not stop with, "Ours is a dirty business but that's what we do," or with the binary positions that can be summed up as either, "Everyone has a right to say whatever he or she wants," or, "If you don't have anything nice to say, don't say anything at all."

Some critics of Goldsmith say that these "works" are not poetry and not worth discussing as poetry. Some say that these are failed poems: ineffective, stupid, misguided, poorly made. Some say that conceptualism is inherently racist and white supremacist.[3]

In a way, the claim by conceptual poets that their intentionally "uncreative" and "unoriginal" writing is apolitical and ahistorical and that all writing is appropriation is not so different from Lowell telling Bishop that "it's oddly enough a technical problem as well as a gentleman's problem" in response to her criticism of Lowell's appropriation of Hardwick's letters. Some conceptual poets say that in a post-truth world, where we know language is only a game, no one should be offended by any kind of poetry. Lyric poets defend the practice of embodying or appropriating the voices and stories of others in the form of dramatic monologues, persona poems, or even "this happened to me and you" narrative poems in which other people appear in either identifiable or unidentifiable ways. What is clear is that these literary actions have hurt others and have set off a wave of argument and discussion about what a person has the right to write about. These debates explore the line between provocation, offense, racism, and harm on both a personal and group level.

■　■　■

3. Cathy Park Hong's essays and letters have done a brilliant job placing Goldsmith's actions and conceptualism in a social and historical context.

My mother's death sparked a traumatic crisis around the question of how my writing might have harmed others, but these questions were there for me long before I wrote *MOTHERs*. Some of these questions may be particularly urgent for me because of my personal history or because of my race, gender, religion, and other aspects of my identity. But I think that, while the answer to these questions might vary from writer to writer, I can't imagine not asking myself: Are there things I should not or would not say? Are there poems or books that step over the line? How so? In what way? Should there be guidelines for writers or for writing as there are for journalists? If there should be guidelines, what should they be?

In a series of lectures called "Discourse and Truth" given at Berkeley in 1983, Michel Foucault outlined the etymology and evolution of the Greek concept of parrhesia from its origins in the Greek tragedies to its denouement in the rise of philosophy. I am not a scholar of literary theory, Greek, or Foucault, but I'm hoping that my translation, even if it is filled with misunderstandings, will move me somewhere useful.

Parrhesia is usually translated into English as "free speech," but our American notion of free speech is so vexed that I would like to go back to a more literal, specific, and less loaded translation.

Here is Foucault:

Etymologically, *"parrhesiazesthai"* means "to say everything"—from *"pan"* [πᾶν] (everything) and *"rhema"* [ῥῆμα] (that which is said). The one who uses *parrhesia*, the *parrhesiastes*, is someone who says everything he has in mind: he does not hide anything, but opens his heart and mind completely to other people through his discourse. In *parrhesia*, the speaker is supposed to give a complete and exact account of what he has in mind so that the audience is able to comprehend exactly what the speaker thinks. . . . In *parrhesia*, the speaker makes it manifestly clear and obvious that what he says is his own opinion. And he does this by avoiding any kind of rhetorical form which would veil what he thinks. Instead, the *parrhesiastes* uses the most direct words and forms of expression he can find.

To imagine poetry as an act of parrhesia, a mode where one "says everything" one has in mind and relays one's own opinion in "the most direct words and forms of expression," is, at first glance, counter to what most of us expect from poetry. We usually expect linguistic refinement rather than directness, obscurity and concision rather than transparency and maximalism. Parrhesia also runs counter to our American notions of freedom, which we usually define as the absence of limitations. In particular, we have strong feelings about freedom of speech, which is a constitutional right limited only when absolutely necessary.

I'm interested in thinking about the poet as a parrhesiastes, or someone who uses parrhesia, because parrhesia has specific requirements, attendant rites, rituals, and qualifications.[4] For "saying everything" to qualify as parrhesia (as opposed to chatter or flattery), there must be a meaningful political purpose to the speech and a significant risk for the speaker.

Foucault:

Someone is said to use *parrhesia* and merits consideration as a *parrhesiastes* only if there is a risk or danger for him or her in telling the truth. For in-

4. In some ways, my entire line of thinking—the search for guidelines and constraints—is not very American. It is also, as I will explain later, not very Christian. But, as a non-Christian, American poet searching for ethical standards, it makes sense to play with this pre-Christian, Western concept in an attempt to develop a code of ethics for writing about real people.

stance, from the ancient Greek perspective, a grammar teacher may tell the truth to the children that he teaches . . . [but] he is not a *parrhesiastes*. However, when a philosopher addresses himself to a sovereign, to a tyrant, and tells him that his tyranny is disturbing and unpleasant because tyranny is incompatible with justice, then the philosopher speaks the truth, believes he is speaking the truth, and, more than that, also takes a risk (since the tyrant may become angry, may punish him, may exile him, may kill him).

Parrhesia is linked to courage in the face of danger: it demands the courage to speak the truth in spite of the potential risk. There must be risk for speech to qualify as parrhesia, but the risk is not always a risk of life. When, for example, you see a friend doing something wrong and you risk incurring his anger by telling him he is wrong, you are acting as a parrhesiastes. If, in a political debate, an orator risks losing his popularity because his opinions are contrary to the majority's opinion or his opinions may usher in a political scandal, he uses parrhesia. Foucault, therefore, translates parrhesia as "fearless speech" rather than "free speech." I like the idea of poetry as "fearless speech," but "fearlessness" in English does not require courage—some people are without fear— and parrhesia requires courage. Perhaps "courageous speech" is, therefore, a more accurate translation.

There must also be a purpose for speech to qualify as parrhesia. Saying you don't like your friend's hairstyle is not an act of parrhesia or courageous speech. Saying your friend's poems are "bullshit eloquence" if you're Rich talking to Lowell probably is. The difference between the two has to do with the inherent political nature and power structure of parrhesia.

"*Parrhesia*," explains Foucault:

is a form of criticism . . . where the speaker . . . is in a position of inferiority with respect to the interlocutor. The *parrhesiastes* is always less powerful than the one with whom he or she speaks. The *parrhesia* comes from "below," as it were, and is directed towards "above." This is why an ancient Greek would not say that a teacher or father who criticizes a child uses *parrhesia*. But when a philosopher criticizes a tyrant, when a citizen criticizes the majority, when a pupil criticizes his or her teacher, then such speakers may be using *parrhesia*.

Here is where our sense of the confessional impulse and parrhesia diverge: the confessional poet is thought of as narcissistic and self-indulgent whereas the parrhesiastes is an underdog hero offering necessary criticism at great risk to herself. Confessional poems are not thought to inspire action or change except as a sort of poetry-as-therapy that, at best, allows the speaker-writer-poet to understand herself better but, more often, is perceived as whining.

I have tried, in my teaching and writing, to reframe our inherited notion of the confessional. I've offered "the confessional" up as a potential source of inspiration and permission for poets wanting to write personal, socially engaged, activist poetry with a sense of real stakes as well as historical context. As I elaborated earlier, however, the word "confessional" is too deeply mired in its connection to Catholicism and hopelessly contaminated by sixty years of critical response that is patriarchal, misogynistic, white supremacist, homophobic, and transphobic, criticism that has simultaneously turned "confessional" into an epithet and a gatekeeping strategy. Confessionalism has at its root the (Christian) practice which imagines that admitting wrongdoing will absolve the confessor from sin, but confessionalism is generally thought of as unethical, in that it violates the privacy of the confessor and disturbs and disrupts the sensibility of the reader. Parrhesia, on the other hand, is inherently political rather than spiritual, does not assume a state of sin, and is considered necessary for the health and well-being of citizens, rulers, and the community.

Foucault:

> A good king accepts everything that a genuine *parrhesiastes* tells him, even if it turns out to be unpleasant for him to hear criticism of his decisions. A sovereign shows himself to be a tyrant if he disregards his honest advisors, or punishes them for what they have said. . . .
>
> . . . Power without limitation is directly related to madness.

The "say everythingness" of confessional poems is often a sign of the poet's madness and/or immorality, but parrhesia is a sign of the speaker's and listeners' sanity and goodness. Years of patriarchal, misogynistic, racist, homophobic critical response to confessional poetry has made liking confessional poetry a sign of one's stupidity, poor taste, madness, and/or immorality. Confessionalism is both a symptom and a cause of the city's (society's) sickness. The "say everythingness" of parrhesia, on the other hand, is essential to the well-being of the city, the success of rulers, and the freedom of individuals.

Of course, the history of the word parrhesia is not without its problems. It arose in a society that practiced slavery and was available, initially, only to citizens of Athens, which included only free men from educated families. I once heard a rabbi explain that trying to practice the laws of Orthodox Judaism today is like trying to use a map of a place that no longer exists to find one's way. That's clearly what I'm doing with parrhesia. I'm not holding up all of ancient Greek society as the one we should strive to emulate. I'm picking and choosing what I want from it, trying to use a map of ancient Athens to navigate modern-day Manhattan. What is useful to me is the notion of a kind of speech that has requirements. In my polis, all human beings are capable of using parrhesia.

So what might the requirements for ethical, "say everything" poetry look like?

1. It tells the truth.

2. It offers the opinion of the poet, and, as such, the poet assumes responsibility for both the content and form of the speech.

3. It punches up and not down.

4. It has a purpose: to ensure the well-being of the city (community) and its inhabitants and to prevent or overthrow tyranny and oppression.

5. Its content engenders significant risk to the speaker.

Whereas confessionalism traffics in shame, parrhesia is speaking truth to power. Parrhesia requires personal risk, but risk is not the same as shame. Whereas confessionalism is inexorably connected to original sin and the fallen nature of man, parrhesia is predicated on understanding and wisdom, on living the way one believes is right and rational. Whereas confessionalism is related to the act of ecclesiastical admission of sin and/or to psychoanalysis (both of which are considered apolitical), parrhesia is always concerned with and directed toward people. Whereas confessionalism serves only the self (and can be self-destructive), parrhesia is oriented toward the benefit of the community (and takes place in the agora, or public space).

The task of writing these lectures forced me to write into the silence that descended upon me (or that I imposed upon myself) after my mother's death, and I've recently composed some of the most boldly confessional poems of my life. I still do not know whether my decision to publish *MOTHERs* and my many confessional-narrative poems are acts of parrhesia or not, but I'm grateful to have worked my way toward a set of ethical guidelines that feels useful to me.

I'm not offended when my work is called confessional, because my writing could not exist without the work of the so-called confessional writers, especially Anne Sexton, Sylvia Plath, and Sharon Olds. On the other hand, I think it is a misunderstanding of my work to think of it only as confessional, which to most people means, simply, writing about oneself. I do write about myself and my life and my lived experience in frank and candid ways, but my poetry is not primarily an act of self-expression. I aspire, instead, to write and publish poems and prose that are communication: aware of the community, relational, political, action-oriented, and, hopefully, ethical. Even though I believe that "narcissism" is often an accusation used to try to control women, I am no longer interested in writing that is only about the self. I have never been very interested in writing that attempts to exist without "self." To write with no self is irresponsible. To write with only self is irrelevant.

■ ■ ■

In "Eve Ewing vs. the Apocalypse," the very first episode of the podcast *VS*, hosts Danez Smith and Franny Choi interview poet, scholar, and community-builder Eve Ewing. Smith asks Ewing, "What are the rules or maybe cautions that you have for writing about people you care about or communities that you care about or issues that you know that are important?" I love Smith's phrase "rules or maybe cautions," and, of course, my ears perked up at the question.

Ewing tells Smith,

When I write about people the three pillars for me are being personal, be-
ing respectful, and being critical. By personal I mean that every single
thing I write about is something that I feel a personal stake in or that I feel
invested in. And then by respectful I mean that I try to talk about people
the way I would want them to talk about me which is that I'm like a full
person, I have a three-dimensional life. . . . I try to use this framing called
desire-based thinking. . . . The third thing is I try to be critical of structures
of power. . . . My job and my desire is to always be challenging the narra-
tive frameworks that are presented to us by people in power. . . . Who has
the power to figure out what narrative is going to dominate? . . . What are
people going to say happened on this day? . . . There's always a narrative
that's coming from the top down.

I love Ewing's three pillars: be personal, be respectful, and be critical.
These pillars overlap with the five rules or cautions I gleaned from my
engagement with Foucault. One might say that Ewing's commitment to
"being personal" includes #2 and #5 above (the poet assumes respon-
sibility for both the content and form of speech and the content engen-
ders significant risk to the poet—there is something personal at stake).
Being respectful might include (but is not exactly the same as) telling
the truth and writing to ensure the well-being of the community. The
third pillar—being critical of power structures and who controls the nar-
rative—is necessary when one is trying to live by #3: punching up, not
down.

In his craft talk "Poetry in the Age of Ferguson, Baltimore and
Charleston," given on June 20, 2015,[5] Roger Reeves elaborates a similar
set of rules and cautions, this time about how to write about violence

5. www.youtube.com/watch?v=QelCu9VjfVs

and brutality, especially state-sanctioned violence. Given three days af-ter a white supremacist terrorist murdered nine African Americans at Emanuel African Methodist Episcopal Church in Charleston, South Carolina, Reeves asks,

> What is the work of poetry in this age of brutality? . . . What shall we ask of the poem, of the story, of the essay? How shall our work encounter, ex-plore, and interrogate these moments, these images? How do we, poets, fiction writers, essayists, write our poems, stories, and essays that engage the political and sociological spectacle of police brutality against black and brown bodies, engage US imperialism, engage neoliberal excess exported as diplomacy and goodwill without reproducing the spectacle, reproduc-ing the wounds of the initial instantiation of violence, without uncritically reproducing what it is we seek to confront and possibly dismantle and sub-vert?

Reeves poses these essential questions about the relationship between art and spectacle and about the responsibility we have as artists for the ways in which we render/re-present violence. Then he looks up from his notes and says he can't help but think about Kenneth Goldsmith's "per-formance" of Michael Brown's autopsy. "How do we become more than 'artful voyeurs,' to borrow Seamus Heaney's phrase from [his poem] 'Punishment'?" asks Reeves, returning to his notes. "What luxuries am I afforded as the writer of the elegy? . . . What privilege am I ignoring?"

Reeves talks about Facebook status updates which "traffic in the spectacle as such." Even if, for example, sharing videos like the one of Eric Garner being choked to death by police is intended to denounce such violence and show solidarity with victims, these kinds of Facebook posts and art that uncritically (and without context) invoke violence (as

Kenneth Goldsmith's "poem" did) *reproduce* violence. Social media reproductions of violence, says Reeves, foreground the sadness/outrage/overwhelmed feelings of the person sharing the videos rather than the real suffering of individuals portrayed. Therefore, says Reeves, these kinds of contextless reproductions of spectacle teach us "how not to make poems."

On the other hand, Heaney's poem "Punishment"—a poem about a woman hanged for adultery whose body the speaker imagines seeing amongst other bodies in a bog—teaches Reeves how to write about violence that is culturally sanctioned and helps Reeves answer the question of how to ethically engage violent imagery.

Heaney's poem is forty-four lines long (eleven quatrains). Here are the last seventeen lines:

> My poor scapegoat,
>
> I almost love you
> but would have cast, I know,
> the stones of silence.
> I am the artful voyeur
>
> of your brain's exposed
> and darkened combs,
> your muscles' webbing
> and all your numbered bones:
>
> I who have stood dumb
> when your betraying sisters,
> cauled in tar,
> wept by the railings,

who would connive
in civilized outrage
yet understand the exact
and tribal, intimate revenge.

"Isn't that a beautiful poem?" Reeves asks. He pauses. One can hear a few assenting murmurs in the audience. Reeves waits. "And that's exactly the trouble and problem of the poem," Reeves says to the audience and to himself.

Heaney, according to Reeves, is keenly aware of this trouble and builds the latter third of "Punishment" to engage the problem of "the making of horror, tragedy, and violence beautiful." According to Reeves, Heaney addresses this problem by calling into question his writerly "position of witness-from-afar," implicating himself in communal violence and drawing our attention to "the art and artificiality of the encounter"—the encounter being, in this case, the poem itself. By implicating himself (and the reader) as a maker, watcher, and perpetrator of violence, Heaney becomes what Reeves calls "a self-conscious and self-critiquing pen." In doing so, Heaney recognizes his poem as a reproduction of violence, what Reeves calls "the second instantiation of violence," and this, according to Reeves, is how Heaney teaches us to become more than "artful voyeurs" as writers and as readers.

The first part of "Punishment" is an erotic description of the dead body of the adulteress. But Heaney doesn't end the poem with this description (doing so would be similar to posting a video of brutality or murder to Facebook or reading Michael Brown's autopsy report). Heaney *looks at* the adulteress, yes, but then, explains Reeves, Heaney *looks in* at his own motivations and subjectivity and *looks out* at the audience/reader(s) and the poem, which is a made thing in conversation with other made things.

"Yet why not say what happened?" Lowell asks in his poem "Epilogue," the last poem in his last book (and one of my favorite poems of his). "We are poor passing facts," writes Lowell, "warned by that to give / each figure in the photograph / his living name."

Like Lowell, I have wanted to "say what happened." Like Olds, I have felt trapped in a closed, suffocating box and tried to write my way out, tried to "say what happened to us / in the lost past." I have tried, in my writing, to say what happened with accuracy, love, rage, and purpose, and have tried to give each figure their "living name." But is it possible to "say what happened" without making violence anew for myself, for my readers, for the people I write about?

Reeves teaches me to ask what luxuries or protections I am afforded as the writer of elegy or poetry of witness or confessional-narrative poems, what privilege(s) I might be ignoring. How might I confront history, especially episodes of brutality, violence, harm, and dehumanization, in an ethical way?

Heaney, says Reeves, "draws our attention to the artifice and artificiality of the encounter and simultaneously to the spectacle of it" in order to show us "the limitedness of his empathy." Americans often bristle at the notion of limits (and several writers expressed offense and irritation at the notion of my wanting to explore guidelines or rules for writing). Creativity, imagination, individuality, and empathy are often described as boundless or immeasurable, transcendent, and outside the purview of ethics. But my imagination, empathy, and ways of seeing and describing are not neutral, unconditional, or limitless. Objectivity is a fallacy or at least a fantasy. Everything I make is imbued with and affected by my subjectivity and positionality.

In order to write ethically, I need to contextualize my poems by thinking about what and whom I'm writing about and why. I need to think about who I am as maker and what I gain by my writing—understanding, money, notoriety, pleasure, power? I need to think, at some point during the writing and publishing of my work, about the "charge" to myself and to others of re-presenting the world, especially when re-rendering harm and when exposing the personal narratives of myself and others. I need to acknowledge that everything I write is on the spectrum of song and betrayal and that to be a poet is to be, as Reeves says, "the purveyor of a second instantiation of violence." I must admit the artifice and artificiality of poems and acknowledge the ways in which I am (inside and outside of poetry) implicated in violence—both personal violence and state violence.

Like many poets today, I am searching for poetry that goes deep, that is disruptive, provocative, offensive, disturbing, high-risk, complex, personal, political, and capable of helping to dismantle oppressive systems, but I also want a poetry that does not harm, reenact violence, or engage in cultural strip-mining. There is no easy solution or formula to the problem of how to write courageously about self and others without harming self and others. As C. D. Wright wrote, "the radical of poetry lies not in the resolution of doubts but in their proliferation."

John Murillo wisely said, poetry "is a dirty business. . . . What's the alternative?" The alternative to poetry isn't staying silent. The opposite of poetry is a sound (or a silence) that is made of the complete absence of doubt, care, caution, and complexity. Ethical guidelines for poets— the five attributes adapted from parrhesia as problematized by Michel

Foucault; Eve Ewing's three pillars; Roger Reeves's "self-conscious and self-critiquing pen"; and so many others I haven't yet touched on—are not commandments, not traffic signs dictating the rules of the road or announcing the distance to destinations, not trail markers painted on trees, and certainly not a set of instructions to avoid being "called out" or "cancelled." I imagine these and other poetry-ethics guidelines as a proliferation of doubts—flickering, persistent, luminescent doubts—fueled, charged, and stoked by brilliant contemporary poet-writer-activist-scholars like Murillo, Ewing, and Reeves. There is no destination, no single, fixed trail or path, no easy way to travel this terrain. But it is helpful to perceive, as fully as possible, everything and everyone around us. I'm grateful for the way these doubts—these poetry radicals—shed light on the understory. Such illuminations help me avoid fatally losing my footing as I make my way amidst the slippery moss, decomposing litter layer, raised roots, saplings of every species, and multitude of human, nonhuman, living, deceased, and imagined beings. Such illuminations might help us mind our step as we wander and explore, hopefully without thoughtlessly, murderously trampling the precious, ever-shifting world around us.

WHY SHE COULD NOT WRITE A LECTURE ON THE POETICS OF MOTHERHOOD

It was thirteen days before she was supposed to deliver a lecture called "The Poetics of Motherhood" at the Portland Literary Arts Center, and she had not written it. She had written parts of it in her head and she had written notes on small pieces of paper that she had misplaced somewhere in the apartment. She was even teaching a class in which she had delivered four mini-lectures in the first four weeks of the semester in preparation to write this lecture, but she had not written the lecture.

She had begun to talk about the lecture here and there, to say things like:

In the poetics of motherhood, if such a thing even exists, Alice Notley, Bernadette Mayer, Toi Derricotte, and other mother-poets wrote into a new space, a space in which they were aware of themselves as mothers, as an underrepresented group, aware that the voices of maker-mothers had not been recorded in the literary record. Sylvia Plath had suicided (1963). Anne Sexton had suicided (1974). Adrienne Rich's *Of Woman Born* came out in 1976. Tillie Olsen's *Silences*, in 1978. The poems that Mayer, Notley, Derricotte, and other mother-poets wrote in the late 1970s should be considered in the context of a mother-poetics, if such a thing exists . . .

She wanted to write about how the experience of motherhood and these poets' identities as mothers had led to formal innovations and new epistemologies, changes in what poems are about, how they look, what they sound like, what they are for, and who they are for.

She was standing in the kitchen talking to James, who had come to help her for the day. She'd texted him the day before: "Hey, sorry to bother you. I'm trying to write a new lecture and my only hope is to try to talk it through with someone and have them type stuff while I talk . . . can't do this alone. Saturday I've got to take Baby Manchild to a soccer game but could do tomorrow morning. Interested? Have time?"

She decided that she would talk through the lecture with James for exactly one hour and, at the end of that hour, she would decide whether it was possible to write this lecture before November 11th. If not, she would cross it off the list. If yes, she would buckle down.

When James arrived Friday morning she told him she'd made her decision. She had to abandon the lecture or at least put off writing it until after her trip to the West Coast, which might mean never writing it. She was trying not to cry in front of James, who was very young and very kind and had been her student. She sat in her son's child-sized wooden chair that made her back ache, across from James, at her kitchen table, rubbing her temples, trying not to cry, and said, "Let's make a list."

James wrote:

1. Prepare for Alicia Ostriker podcast conversation—TODAY! 2 p.m.
2. Record Shane McCrae intro & outro

3. Finish writing Steph Burt intro & outro

4. Return RZ boots to Zappos

5. Find hand-me-down boots in basement storage for Baby Manchild's overnight class trip

6. Find keys to basement storage

7. Text Josh for combo code for locker in basement storage

8. Locate Kristin Prevallet's books

9. Confirm Prevallet's class visit

10. Submit undergrad midterm grades

11. RSVP to ping-pong birthday party of what's-his-name for Baby Manchild

12. Gather art supplies for in-class poetry exercises 11/8

13. Get bags of rice for in-class exercise 11/8

14. Upload sound files from Bernadette Mayer interview

15. Return adapter to NYU and purchase own

16. Find *We Were Feminists Once* and read it before 11/10

The list of what she did not tell James:

1. The night before, she had been crying, and her husband had said something to her—she thinks what he said was, "The family can't function with you working so hard," but it's possible she misheard him. She had been expecting him to say she shouldn't work this hard, had long suspected that's what he thought *the big problem was*—her work. It would not be the first time she'd misheard a man telling her what the big problem was, but whatever he had actually said, she had heard: "The family can't function with you working so hard."

2. She felt like crying and was having trouble making a list without crying.

3. She was considering whether she might be able to write her lecture as a series of lists but suspected she needed to give up on the whole idea of writing a new lecture before her trip to Portland, no matter what form the lecture might eventually take.

Triage.

On Thursday, her son had been rubbing his temples and trying not to cry. He was overwhelmed by having to apply to college, by his homework, by the fact that he had lost several hours of work on his *Hamlet* paper because of a computer malfunction and because he was staying up too late every night obsessively checking fivethirtyeight.com and reading articles on the election and had come to believe that "men are bad" and was struggling to write 650 words about a situation in which he had failed and what he had learned from that experience. Maybe, he thought, he should just put everything else aside and memorize the *Hamlet* soliloquy because what he really cared about was the opinion of his English teacher who was very brilliant but not very understanding and thought that the overemphasis on college applications could be counterbalanced by assigning an inordinate amount of homework fall semester of senior year.

"Triage," she told her son. "Do you know what triage is?"

She explained the prioritizing that doctors did in emergency rooms and during medical emergencies and told him he had to do triage and attend to one thing at a time, and together they reordered his to-do list and sat together until he had done the first four things on the list.

That is what she did on Thursday instead of writing about the poetics of motherhood.

Also dinner, also office hours, also finally buying herself new boots from Zappos because the old ones had a hole in the sole and her socks kept getting wet.

What she did not tell James: her lecture on the poetics of motherhood was bleeding out. It was unlikely to survive no matter what kind of care it received. It was bleeding out or it was "walking wounded." Either way, it was still not her most pressing problem and, therefore, never next on the list.

What she did not tell James: the family was broken, and she did not know who to help first or how and she feared they would not make it through intact. She felt she was constantly attending to the wrong person in the wrong way.

What she did not tell James: she was not sure if the consequences—rage, resentment, frustration—of abandoning her lecture were greater than the consequences of buckling down and writing the lecture at any cost. Also: she did not like the phrase "buckling down."

James waited politely, not looking at her.

In a few hours, she was going to interview the critic, professor, feminist mother-poet Alicia Ostriker for the podcast she should not have started and which she could not seem to stop, so instead of telling James about triage, she and James made a list of questions for Alicia, which ended up only being one question:

1. I'm supposed to give this lecture, "The Poetics of Motherhood," in less than two weeks, but I have not had a chance to write it mostly because of family responsibilities and teaching commitments. Maybe I will end up writing it after my lectureship is over, maybe not, but I was hoping we could talk about it for a few minutes. I want to talk about women poets such as you, Alice Notley, Toi Derricotte, Bernadette Mayer, and

Lucille Clifton. It's my understanding that after Adrienne Rich's book *Of Women Born* and Tillie Olsen's book *Silences* there was a real sense that mothers were an underrepresented voice in art and, in particular, in poetry. It seems to me that there has been some good work done to look at the poems by Notley, Mayer, you, Derricotte, Clifton, Jordan, Lorde as part of the women's movements and the Black Arts Movement, but I haven't seen a lot of writing about the way in which the experience of motherhood affected the work and poetics of your generation of mother-writers. Your books *Stealing the Language* and *Writing Like a Woman* are the most important texts to me, in terms of raising awareness about the gendered nature of poetry, language, and criticism. I think my lecture was going to be my attempt to make some observations about what it meant, particularly in the late '70s, to be writing *like a mother*. Am I off base? Was your experience as a mother, not just as a woman, relevant to your poetics?

She and James found *We Were Feminists Once* by Andi Zeisler, who she was planning to interview on November 10th in Portland, Oregon. They found Kristin Prevallet's books. They found the keys for the basement, the code for the padlock, and, in the storage unit: a box of boys' clothes and shoes she'd been storing for eight years, and, in that box, she found the pair of size three, barely used winter boots that Baby Manchild needed for his school overnight.

"Now can I talk about the lecture?" she asked.

"Of course," James said.

She put her face in her hands.

"Let's look for my notes," she said.

"OK," James said.

All they could find was an empty, opened envelope on the microwave that said:

POETICS OF MOTHERHOOD

motherhood = "powerless responsibility" —Adrienne Rich.

→ the way my gender is complicated by having male children?

→ [Mary Shelley

At the very end of September she had gone away for the weekend to write her lecture on the poetics of motherhood. She had made lists and notes and had called her friend and collaborator, her poetry-sister, Arielle Greenberg, to talk the lecture through. She had said, "I want to talk about how Notley and Mayer and Ostriker and Derricotte's work have innovative markers, means, and forms." She was thinking of Mayer's book-length poem, *Midwinter Day,* written in 1978, and Mayer's earlier durational projects, like *Memory* and *Studying Hunger,* and Alicia Ostriker's *The Mother/Child Papers* and Toi Derricotte's book-length poem, *Natural Birth,* and about how these works could only be fully appreciated in the context of these women writing about and during their lived experience as mothers. She was thinking about the ways in which these works were long and messy and relational and exceedingly interrupted and interruptible. Also: indeterminacy. She wrote "indeterminacy" on many scraps of paper and then lost them somewhere in the apartment. She was thinking about how these works often included lists and questions and domestic details, sometimes fascinating, sometimes boring, like what people ate, what the children were doing, what the children were saying. She was thinking about the ways in which these works subverted patriarchal ideals of what poems and art should be—concise, condensed, linear, rhetorical, lyrical. These poems were durational, cyclical or phasic, and radically inclusive. The departure of these poems from previously held ideals of what poems should sound like and look like and do had to be understood within the context of having been made by women writing about motherhood while mothering young children and while searching for new forms in which to tell stories that had not been told before.

"OK," said Arielle, "this is good. I haven't really heard any of this before, not in this way. But I think you need to focus. You need to narrow down what you're talking about to a few poets. And narrow down what you want to say about them."

She had gone away that weekend at the end of September to write her lecture, but she needed to prepare for class and, in order to prepare for class, she had to read the book-length poem that one of her students had written for workshop in response to the four mini-lectures she had given about motherhood. The student's poem was shocking and amazing. It was more and differently unsettling than anything she'd ever read in workshop, maybe more shocking and amazing than anything she'd read ever. The poem included many concerning details—history of trauma, abuse, self-harm, mental illness, body issues, self-doubt, depression. The poem asked over and over for the reader to worry about the author. The poem was ashamed of its own urgent alarm, of what it meant to ask the reader to worry. The poem shocked, provoked, and then doubted and questioned its own shockingness, its own provocations. The poem problematized truth, autobiography, and the relationship between author and reader. She worried. She cared deeply for this student. She had lost a student two years earlier to suicide. She worried.

On the first day of class she had said, "Write down as many associations as you can with the word 'mother.' Put the five associations that surprise you or interest you most on the board. Circle the ones that are 'hot' or that seem like they would spark writing for you."

In the second class, she had written on the whiteboard:

FREE WRITING —5 minutes (we will not share aloud)

What do you know about your own birth?
What do you know about birth?
What famous birth stories do you know?
What archetypes of birth do you know?
What are your associations around birth?

In the third class, she had written on the whiteboard:

QUESTIONS TO CONSIDER —10 minutes (we will not share aloud)

What is the most transformational event you've had in your life?
In this event, were you the one "giving birth" or "being born"?
What are the things in your life that are ritualized?
How are you being enculturated?
How is your sexuality controlled or compartmentalized?
What are your feelings about death, birth, connection, aging, bodily trans-
    formation?

In the fourth class, she had written:

FREEWRITING —5 minutes (we will not read these aloud)

How are you cared for?
How strong are you?

How much help do you need?

What has been the most challenging experience of your life?

What is your experience of greatest becoming?

Of othering?

What in your life has prepared you for the next hard thing?

Are your obstacles primarily personal, familial, psychological, governmental, financial, institutional?

What are your strengths?

And, after these freewritings, she had given four mini-lectures about the topic "mother" and asked the students to write a poem that responded to these mini-lectures in whatever way they wanted. And now here was this poem. It was book-length. It was longer than book-length. It was ninety-three pages. It was unlike anything she'd ever read. It was not what she had expected and yet she could not help berating herself, asking herself, What did you expect? What did you expect with all that freewriting? All that talk about mothers?

But the poem was extraordinary, and she had read an earlier draft of it and had talked with the student about whether or not the student was prepared for the consequences of sharing such a poem with the class. Was the student in therapy? Was the student well enough to be this vulnerable in class? They had decided, together, that the student should share this longer-than-book-length poem with the class, but still, she worried.

A few hours after the poem went out via email, another student emailed her and asked to speak to her on the phone. This student wanted to talk about the ethics of responding to such a provocative and worrisome poem as a piece of art rather than as a matter of emotional exigency and personal safety. So, instead of writing her lecture on the poetics of motherhood, she had reread the student's poem and had called a friend about it and had called another workshop instructor. Instead of writing her lecture on the poetics of motherhood she had spoken to the concerned student on the phone and tried to be honest but reassuring and had said, "I cannot promise you that nothing will happen to X. What I can say is that your response is normal and appropriate. X's poem inspires discomfort in any caring, empathetic reader and forces the question of how one should respond. I want to normalize your response and give you permission to be honest about that response and also go on with your own life knowing that you are not responsible for X's well-being and that the decision to share this work with the class was made by X and myself knowing it might upset others. While I cannot promise you that X will be alright, I can promise you that I have more responsibility than you do and I am working with X and I think the decision to share this piece is a healthy one."

Triage. She had put the notes on her lecture away to reread the student's poem. She had sent the writer of the poem an email to check in. She had followed up by email with the concerned student-reader. She had made a list of the process exercises they would do in class after they were finished with the next three weeks of workshop, including counting rice, making self-portraits while looking in mirrors, writing poems together in pairs alternating one word at a time, making a phone call to someone who had died in the privacy of the upstairs office and recording the audio.

"If I manage to write this lecture," she told James, "I will give it in Portland, Oregon, on my mother's birthday, which is November 11th."

James nodded.

"And there will be a female president-elect," she told James. "Not only the first female president, but the first *mother* president," she told James.

James nodded.

In August, she had decided she was going to write a new lecture, one more lecture that she would give in Portland, Oregon, on November 11th, her mother's birthday, just after the election of the new, first, mother president-elect, and that she would write about the poetics of motherhood. She had also, in August, decided that she did not want to teach her graduate workshop and her advanced undergraduate workshop in the same-old-same-old way because she was sick of the way workshops lead to a conformity of response and a reiteration of the values she had begun to see as cis-hetero-patriarchal and white supremacist. She did not want students to bring in poems that tried to conform to received notions of excellence or for the students to try to please her with their poems. She wanted them to write the poems *only they* could write. She wanted these poems to resist conformity of all kinds and for the poems to delight, surprise, please, enrage, and maybe deeply confuse her. She wanted the students to write poems that required the invention of new critical language. Honestly, she didn't even care what poems they wrote. What she really wanted was for the students to explore and develop sustainable practices that they could use to write for years and years, for the rest of their lives.

"After careful consideration and tremendous thought we have settled on NOT doing the new lecture (this could change)," James wrote on the to-do list.

She had considered trying to write the lecture on the poetics of motherhood as a series of to-do lists, but, in order to do so, she needed to make it through the first of many items on the many to-do lists she kept making and misplacing.

In October, she and her husband had gone back to Portland, Maine, away from the kids, not just to be together but to *be together*, and she thought perhaps she would be able to finally begin writing her lecture on the poetics of motherhood because her husband had so many papers to grade. But her husband's grandfather had died, and they had had to return home early so her father-in-law who was watching their kids could return to Los Angeles. Then, a few days later, she and the husband and their sons flew to Los Angeles for her husband's grandfather's funeral. She thought perhaps she would, on the plane there or the plane back, be able to begin to write her lecture on the poetics of motherhood, but, when they got there, the husband entered a removed dimension he went to when experiencing emotional duress, and each time they got into the rented minivan everyone started yelling or cursing or crying or gripping the wheel or listening to headphones, and this meant that she was triage triage triage clenching her jaw and not sleeping and feeling alone in the midst of too many and definitely not writing about the poetics of motherhood.

"What are some of the things you might use to approach a topic?" she had asked her class, and together they had made a list:

* Memory
* Storytelling
* Etymology
* History
* Persona
* Autobiography

* Formal interpretation

* Association

* Research

One son was worried about his college applications and felt guilty for worrying at a time like this. One was angry and wouldn't look at her or talk to her except to yell at her. One was stuck in a loop of worrying and worrying about death: his own, hers, his father's, everyone's.

"Papa lived a long life," she told the death-obsessed one. "He had a large, loving family. He was a success in all he did. He was loved. He will be missed because, when he was alive, he was so present in everyone's life."

The boy cried.

"There are things worse than death," she told the boy.

He cried.

She held him.

On the airplane on the way to LA she had answered emails and made lists until the boy needed for her to hold his hand, which made typing impossible. So she held his hand and read a book called *Motherhood Reconceived* by Lauri Umansky.

"It's really bad timing, Mom," her son had said, in late October, about his college applications, "that you've been gone for three weekends in a row. I need more help."

"Prioritize your marriage," her therapist had said before and after the trip to LA.

A book said, Feminism . . .

A book said, Birth poses a major conceptual threat to male dominance.

A book said, Our society remains strongly patriarchal yet pays increasing lip service to the ideal of equality. Since growing numbers of women espouse this idea, our culture will not survive in its present form unless these women can also be made to internalize the basic tenets of the technocratic model of reality. This dilemma is one of the most intriguing: how to get women, in a culture that purports to hold gender equality as an ideal, to accept a belief system that inherently denigrates them?

A book said, To apply statistics to herself a woman must depersonalize her own experience. Depersonalization (in communication as well as in medical practice) can only lead to alienation.

She made a list of dates. She made notes about feminism. Notes about the women's movement. She learned to say "women's movements" instead of "women's movement."

She copied down this quote from C. D. Wright to read in class:

Poetry and mothering are symbiotic—the relationship is close, protracted, and not necessarily of benefit one to the other. They are different organisms, different species. There are certainly periods when they fill each other up, and there are just as certainly periods when they drain each other's cup. It is not my choice to forego one for the other. I was asked by a poet who reluctantly chose not to have children what conditions I would require to become the best poet I could. And I had to allow, I had them, though I struggle for the opportunities to enter that clearing where I am alone and afraid and humbled and pregnant only with the anticipation of thinking, dreaming, creating, writing without interruption. I had to allow, I require the distraction, that I require the attachment, and that unencumbered I merely dissipate; I come undone. I admit, I require the struggle though it brings me to my knees when I most long to be standing free.

"What part of you feels better when you don't exercise #JustCurious," her friend texted her, the same friend she had said she would go walking with every single day, the friend she no longer walked with because each morning when she was supposed to be writing her lecture on the poetics of motherhood she was preparing for class or answering emails or taking her son to soccer games or sitting at the kitchen table making to-do lists with her other son or looking for the book that the new couple's therapist had recommended that she could not find and should not be reading but *should* be reading according to the new couple's therapist.

Somewhere Marina Abramović was counting rice. She wanted to count rice but she needed to buy rice to give to her students so they could count rice, which was one of the assignments she was going to give them now that she was not teaching workshop same-old-same-old.

She sat in the uncomfortable, designed-for-a-child, wooden chair and told James about how, when she'd gone to interview Bernadette Mayer for the podcast she should not be making but couldn't stop making, she had offended Bernadette by asking the question her writer-sister Arielle had told her to ask. She'd asked Bernadette about writing the feminist epic *Midwinter Day* and she'd tried to ask her what it was like to be in what she and Arielle hoped would be a period of new creativity and wisdom—a postmenopausal stage which was called, by some, "the crone stage." Her mother had died. Arielle's mother had died. They wanted to know if life in one's sixties and seventies was joyful, sensual, meaningful, enjoyable. They hoped it was. They wanted to know what it was like to write when one was not mothering young children or teenagers. But when she had used the word "crone," Bernadette had said, "Are you asking me what it's like to be old and ugly? You'd better go across the road and ask my neighbor; she's much older and uglier than I am!"

James smiled. He looked down at the to-do list. All they had done was find Baby Manchild's boots, write up a list of questions which was only one question, and decide that she would not, after all, try to write her lecture on the poetics of motherhood, at least not by November 11th.

She had seen *Midwinter Day* written about in terms of capitalism, documentary poetics, the 1970s "dematerialization of the art object," and in comparison to James Joyce's *Ulysses* (both start with the same word), but she had never seen it explored as an example of the poetics of motherhood. She had a list of words she had seen people use to describe Mayer's *Midwinter Day*: quotidian, encyclopedic, catalogue, feminist. She had found a Post-it note on her desk that had been serving as a coaster for a mug that had once held the single shot of espresso she allowed herself every morning, never after 10 a.m. It read:

[[MIDWINTER DAY: quotidienne, encyclopaedic, catalogue, feminism (sources?)]]

WRITING / MOTHERING AS A SITE OF CONFLICT
→ A metaphor for an "interrupted life"
→ For any kind of family/personal life and "work"
→ What it means to choose one's work OVER one's child.
   (And to be thrown back into the position of the child.)

INCLUSIVITY—of the body, of poop, of that which is preverbal or not verbal
   Ask students! Make a list of people who have mothered you. Make a list of nonhuman things that have mothered you. Create a definition of "mothering" by looking at that list, by trying to include (without flattening) all the people and things you've included.

She told James that, when talking to Bernadette—having driven three hours to see her at her home in upstate New York, having bought a blue Smith-Corona electric (not electronic) typewriter for Bernadette as a present on eBay as well as bialys (not bagels) and two packages of smoked salmon—she'd tried wildly to backtrack and started speechifying about how that's not what she'd meant by "crone." She'd meant, you know, like how the older sense of "virgin" wasn't a woman who'd never had sex but was a woman who "belonged to herself" (like the goddess Athena), but Bernadette had shouted, "A virgin is a woman who's never had sex!" And so she had tried to get out of that line of questioning as fast as she could, but never quite recovered, and had, after the recorded conversation, had a blazing fight with her husband, a huge bonfire of a fight, and had barely slept a wink in the overpriced bed-and-breakfast bed, and the next morning they drove home a day early to stand in the rain and watch their youngest son lose in round three of the Brooklyn Italians' Columbus Day Cup rather than spend the day *together* in the quaint, industrial town of Hudson.

"You haven't eaten lunch," said James. "And soon it's time to go talk to Alicia. I'm worried you won't have time to eat." Eating lunch was on the list, and it was 1 p.m.

In August, she had posted to the poet-moms listserv to ask for advice. She had written, "Who are the great mother-poets? I'm trying to write a lecture on the poetics of motherhood even though I don't know what I mean by that yet and probably won't until I start writing. Also, I'm sick of teaching workshop the way I've always taught it. Does anyone have any new, great ideas?"

C had written back, "Call me," so she had spoken on the phone with C, a great mother-poet-teacher who said she was also sick of the standard workshop model. She decided, therefore, to do what great mother-poet-teacher C did in her class, which was to lecture on a topic—any topic—for four weeks while each student wrote a poem that was at least eight pages long (at some point in the composition process) in response (loosely defined) to the four weeks of lecturing and then workshop these poems for the next three weeks. This approach would help instill in the students an appreciation for research, for deep engagement in a topic rather than the shorter one-off poems traditional workshops so often inspired. She decided that in the first four weeks she would deliver four mini-lectures about "motherhood" and that at the end of this time she would go away for three days at the very end of September and write her lecture about the poetics of motherhood, come hell or high water.

She had reread Adrienne Rich. She had reread Tillie Olsen. She made lists of mother-poets and poems about motherhood. She had made a timeline of the important events of the women's movements. She had reread Sharon Olds, Lucille Clifton, Alice Notley, Bernadette Mayer, June Jordan, Audre Lorde, Joy Harjo, Brenda Hillman, Toi Derricotte, Rita Dove. She had reread *Stealing the Language, Writing Like a Woman, The Grand Permission,* and *Mother Reader.* She had read essays by Jane Smiley, Virginia Woolf, Jane Lazarre, Joy Katz, Brenda Shaughnessy, Belle Boggs, Susan Briante. She watched *Jeanne Dielman* by Chantal Akerman. She watched *Baby Cobra* with Ali Wong.

She had scanned or linked to the following poems or excerpts of texts and then uploaded these to the website she made for her class:

"When We Dead Awaken," Adrienne Rich
"Professions for Women," Virginia Woolf
"A Wild Surmise: Motherhood and Poetry," Alicia Ostriker

"One Out of Twelve: Women Who Are Writers in Our Century," Tillie
Olsen

"The Damnation of Women," Tillie Olsen

"Can Mothers Think?" Jane Smiley

Sharon Olds: "The Fear of Oneself," "Satan Says," "Beyond Harm," "I
Could Not Tell," "The Language of the Brag," "I Go Back to May 1937"

Lucille Clifton: "the lost baby poem," "the thirty eighth year"

Alice Notley: "The Prophet," "A Baby Is Born Out of a White Owl's Fore-
head"

Brenda Shaughnessy: "Liquid Flesh," "Our Andromeda"

Natural Birth, Toi Derricotte

"Here Happy Is No Part of Love," Rachel Zucker

"The Rejection of Closure," Lyn Hejinian

"The Yellow Wallpaper," Charlotte Perkins Gilman

"Baby Poetics," Joy Katz

"Hunger," Adrienne Rich

"The Art of Waiting," Belle Boggs

"Mother is Marxist," Susan Briante

Midwinter Day, Bernadette Mayer

"The Lyric 'I' Drives to Pick Up Her Children from School: A Poem in the Post-
Confessional Mode," Olena Kalytiak Davis

"Mighty Forms," Brenda Hillman

Alice Notley: "Your Dailiness," "White Phosphorus," "The Prophet"

Alicia Ostriker: "The Leaf Pile," "Propaganda Poem: Maybe for Some
Young Mamas"

"The Double Image," Anne Sexton

Sylvia Plath: "Morning Song," "Fever 103°"

The Grand Permission, Brenda Hillman and Patricia Dienstfrey, eds.

Beyond the Whiteness of Whiteness, Jane Lazarre

Jeanne Dielman, Chantal Akerman

Audre Lorde: "Black Mother Woman," "Now That I Am Forever with Child"

"Night Feeding," Muriel Rukeyser

"Spelling," Margaret Atwood

Susan Griffin: "I Like to Think of Harriet Tubman," "The Bad Mother"

"Ain't I a Woman?" Sojourner Truth

"Well," said James, "you have all of next Monday and Tuesday free . . . if no one comes to your office hours."

"Ha," she said.

She knew she could give one of the other lectures in Portland. She could talk about the poetics of wrongness, her first lecture, which she had written mostly because her sons constantly thought and told her she was wrong, her husband thought and told her she was wrong, and her editor thought and told her she was wrong, and she felt so wrong she felt herself sinking and sinking into wrongness and realized poetry was always a place she had gone to when she felt wrong or wronged, not to feel better and, no, not to feel *right*, but to be in wrongness in some right relation, and she knew she had always felt this and had learned this from Allen Ginsberg and Adrienne Rich and Alice Notley. She could give that lecture, but the truth was that nothing, *nothing* could compare with the feeling of brokenness and terror she felt when she felt she had not been a good enough mother, and this was her poetics of wrongness. No, this was her poetics of *motherhood*. Nothing could compare to the feeling of ambivalence and rage she felt when torn between her mothering and her art, and this was her poetics of motherhood, and she wanted to write about that.

She could talk about the history of confessional poetry, about the misogyny and white supremacy and cis-centric heteronormativity and Christian-centeredness of the confessional impulse, especially the critical misogyny leveled against Plath and Sexton. This lecture had arisen out of trying to come to terms with the confessional epithet leveled against her and from trying to come to terms with the legacy of Sexton and Plath, two mother-poets who had taken their own lives. What might it entail to claim their mantle and what might it mean to reject it? Also, what might it mean to claim Sharon Olds, maligned though also beprized, as the mother she might want or the mother she might want to be? To come to terms with the fact that she would never be Jorie Graham, never be Alice Notley, never be Bernadette Mayer, and why the hell was she constantly, constantly searching for a mother and for the mother she wanted to be? This was her poetics. And it was a poetics of motherhood.

She could talk about the ethical consequences of writing about real people: her husband, her children, her mother, her friends. About how she had gone to Foucault and several contemporary poets to develop her own set of ethical guidelines, which she promptly broke in the poems she wrote while struggling to write the lecture about ethics, the poems that were hyperconfessional and full of shame and trespass and which broke every self-imposed guideline she'd suggested, every guideline which, if one were paying any attention at all, implied one should not write about those who cannot give consent. But to adhere to that ethical standard was to never write about one's children or about motherhood, which was to go back to a poetics that did not include the voices of mothers or the lives of mothers or the bodies and spirits and complex desires and sexualities and rage and ambition and boredom and ferocity and passion of mothers! And that to espouse a pre-motherhood poetics would mean erasing every word she'd ever written, erasing herself! But to write one single word more (which she had done and was doing) knowing how deep this trespass was, knowing full well the harm she had caused—death even (her own mother's *death!*)—and the harm she might be causing her own children, this was her poetics of motherhood.

On Tuesday, a bright-eyed student came to her office hours to talk about "vernacular criticism" and "the poetics of excess." These were the student's phrases, although "vernacular criticism" might have come from Eileen Myles. She couldn't remember because she was too busy repeating the student's phrases to herself, thinking, "Yes—vernacular criticism!—that is the name of what I want to do," and, "Oh! Perhaps I am not writing and not not-writing about the poetics of motherhood but am instead not writing about the poetics of excess!" The bright-eyed student wanted her to read a piece of vernacular criticism about the poetics of excess, but she said no, she could not read anything until after she had returned from her trip where she might or might not be giving a new lecture that she had not yet written. The bright-eyed student looked profoundly disappointed but said she understood, don't worry, she was signed up for office hours the next week and the next and the next, through the end of the semester.

Also, she told James, she needed to do much more serious reading and thinking about the emergence of Language poetry. And it was important to not only have examples of bio-mothers or cis women mothers. Also what about Rachel Blau DuPlessis? Lyn Hejinian? Where was that amazing quote she had copied down in which Rachel Blau DuPlessis talks about being an adoptive mother and writing her long poem "Writing," in which she typeset and handwrote text. . . . Something about periods as punctuation and menses and also about the whole idea of marginality? And now that she thought about it, she couldn't think of a single book she'd read about transmotherhood or by a transmother.

"It's almost time for you to go to Alicia's," James said. "You haven't eaten."

"OK, OK," she said.

She opened the refrigerator and found the jelly and peanut butter. Her mother had been very beautiful and very thin and had not cared very much about food and had not been very interested in creating regular routines, especially when these interfered with her writing and performing. All throughout her childhood, when she was hungry, her mother would offer peanut butter and jelly at any time of day or night. That, and only that. And sometimes her mother would eat that and only that herself rather than stop working. Unlike her mother, she took great pride in the meals she made for her three sons and husband but knew, when her mother was alive, her mother had thought this was a waste of time, time that would be better spent writing, although her mother had later in her life become an extremely picky eater and demanded her daughter cook complicated meals for her as a matter of course.

The jam—there was only a little bit left in the jar, and she was annoyed that her son had put it back in the refrigerator after using it that morning—was covered in white mold.

"Oh," she said.

"What?" James asked.

She told him. She showed him. Then she told James the story of why she had dropped out of a PsyD program when her second son was a newborn and her oldest son was eighteen months old. The story involved not noticing that her oldest had thrown up during the night, having woken at 4 a.m. to feed him—she'd been nursing the newborn all night and was worried about the two-hour commute to Rutgers with the new-born, which often involved having to pull over on the New Jersey Turn-pike to nurse as cars and trucks hurtled by. She had put her eighteen-month-old, bottle-fed and asleep, back into the vomit-covered crib without noticing the vomit and later that day received a nasty note from the day care center after the husband (who had also not noticed the vomit, even in the light of day) had dressed the boy and taken him to day care, a small clump of vomit in the boy's hair.

The vomit crib. Nursing in the back of a car on the New Jersey Turn-pike. Taking a semester off, taking two semesters off because one had to do these courses in sequence and pick up where one had left off no mat-ter the circumstances of needing to take a semester off, bringing the eighteen-month-old (who was then twenty-seven months old) and her newborn (who was then nine months old) to a new day care where none of the teachers knew about the vomit crib, leaving the babies there for their first full day, which was Tuesday, September 11, 2001, watching the second plane hit the tower, the sky fill with smoke, the smell—she would never go back to Rutgers. How could she leave these babies in a city covered with the emotional fallout of death and despair? This was her poetics of motherhood.

Alice Notley: "There was no poetry that corresponded to my expe-rience; there was no poetry with motherhood as its subject. I had my first child in 1972, and there was virtually nothing there in the poetry to help me know who I was."

She ate the peanut butter sandwich, no jelly. She wondered, as she ate it, if her son would become ill from having eaten mold-covered jam. She thought, This is why I cannot write a lecture on the poetics of motherhood, because the jam is covered in mold, because she had not noticed, because her son had eaten it.

That summer, she had made notes for her mini-lectures for her workshop that could surely, without much effort, be transformed into the lecture on the poetics of motherhood.

The mini-lecture notes said:

If we assume that the following is true: artists and makers have largely been men or, more recently and only in much smaller numbers, childless women, and that without the stories and language and arts and thinking that would have been developed by mothers, we have a limited variety of voices, forms, archetypes for human experience. What does it mean, then, that in the 1970s there was an emergence of mother-voices and an awareness and exploration of the consequences of the historical paucity of mother-voices?

Are there any "unifying" elements of mother-voice, such as:
   * Continuity, subversion of the patriarchy
   * Subversion of dualities: mind/body; sacred/profane; wisdom/knowledge; magic/science; mind/body, magic/science, high art/craft of male/female
   * Negotiations of the needs of self and other
   * Transformation of body and self through the highly ritualized space of culture
   * Complex relationship toward feminism/womanhood
   * New epic/Staying but not like Penelope
   * Relationship to the unknown

* Resistance to oppression in all forms

* Resistance to technocratic model: more information and less experience

* Subversion of adrenaline and of testosterone. The poetics of oxytocin, the "stay-and-play" hormone. What would it look like to write with oxytocin? (essentialist? trans-exclusionary?)

* "Third space" of motherhood

* Motherhood as an inescapable education on attachment, nurturing, and separation

Her notes said: Time *bends* as the mother (male or female or fluid) relives or reexperiences an early age through close contact with and care of an infant, baby, child, adolescent and simultaneously inhabits her own past-future as the mother identifies with the child and with the mother's own mother, as she is now the mother.

She found several more Post-its and torn envelopes and strips of scratch paper. One said: Mother as a site of **looking for one's origins**.

One said:

THE NOT-MOTHER CATEGORY

* By choice (Molly Peacock) . . . reread *Paradise, Piece by Piece*
* By biology (infertility)
* By politics
* By economics
* By institutionalized racism

One said: Sally Mann's motherhood creates a necessary site of ethical conflict that is not just about mothers.

Jane Smiley: "It means something, then, if mothers never speak in a literary voice, and if their sense of themselves as mothers and their view of those around them is not a commonplace of our written culture. It means, for one thing, that everyone in the culture is allowed, or even encouraged, to project all their conflicting fantasies, wishes, and fears onto the concept of motherhood, and onto their individual mothers and wives, which in turn creates of motherhood an ever-changing kaleidoscope of unrealistic and often conflicting aspirations and roles."

Also, she told James, she was afraid. She was afraid to write the lecture on the poetics of motherhood because too many of the women she was talking about were white. The black mother-poets, except Toi Derricotte—Lucille Clifton, June Jordan, Audre Lorde, Rita Dove—seemed to be doing something else in their poems. Their poems were shorter, more direct, urgent in ways that made Mayer and Notley, with their long, rambling, domestic, epic anti-epics—their chattiness—seem like maybe she was not actually observing a poetics of motherhood but was observing a poetics of white cis-hetero motherhood. Was this poetics of excess actually a poetics of privilege? If she failed to talk more about the structural, lived inequalities—single motherhood, income disparities, etc.—that made balancing a writing practice with mothering exponentially more difficult for black women and queer women, was she going to reinscribe racism and homophobia like the straight, white second-wave feminists had done when they tried and failed to "invite" black women and lesbians into "their" movement? If she did not do the real work of untangling race and gender, and maybe even if she did, she was going to reinscribe racism and the damage done by white feminists to black feminists and by straight feminists to lesbian feminists and this she did not want.

She felt that this problem could be partially solved if she asked Isaac what he thought and, more importantly, if she reread Sonia Sanchez.

She suspected that in the work of Sanchez was the key to an observation of motherhood that was diverse and inclusive and complex and beautiful, but she had not had time, and what about Latina and Asian American and Indigenous mothers? Not having time was no excuse at all. At the same time, not having time was perhaps the single most unifying aspect of the poetics of motherhood.

So she tried to explain this thing about time being the most unifying aspect of the poetics of motherhood to Isaac, who had also been her student, who was now becoming a great scholar and poet and had a kind and gentle way of chastising her. Isaac replied:

"It might be useful to think through how the experience of 'not having enough time' is not evenly distributed across all mothers and how, historically, the labor of women of color/denial of their roles as mothers (especially black women) has made possible the ability of white mothers to inhabit the category of motherhood (even as inhabiting that category is itself exploitative/hierarchized)."

Oh yes, of course, she had thought. Yes! How much of what she thought could be a poetics of motherhood was just another codification of the protection of white women, which was one of the greatest weapons of white supremacy? How could she talk about motherhood without talking about rape, institutionalized gender violence, compulsory motherhood, slavery, and what a book called the construction of the "inviolability of black women" and the construction of the "hyperviolability of white women"? What about the ways in which the criminal punishment system, incarceration, especially convict leasing and chain gangs, lead to the un-womaning of black women, the un-mothering of black women? The denial of motherhood as a category to black mothers—and why had Sonia Sanchez not been on her list from the beginning?

Adrienne Rich had written that the institution of motherhood "aims at ensuring that that potential [to become a mother]—and all women—shall remain under male control"—yes, indeed! But when Rich had written "[the institution of motherhood] has alienated women from our bodies by incarcerating us in them," well, there is a very big difference between being incarcerated in your body and having your body incarcerated.

Even if she had *time*—even if she had the kind of time that (only?) a kind of white woman like her could have—how could she make claims about a unifying aspect of motherhood when motherhood was a category often denied to women who were mothers and when the range of experiences among mothers of different races, classes, sexual orientations, gender identities, and gender expressions was so diverse? Was she trying to make a coalition poetics but failing to heed Audre Lorde's exhortation that "the master's tools will never dismantle the master's house"?

She had tried to explain to her students about "&vs.,"[1] which is pronounced "andverse," a newly invented form of punctuation meant to destabilize binary modes of thinking and encourage dialectical understanding. She had hoped that a poetics of motherhood might help her understand self &vs. other, but maybe it was more accurate to say motherhood &vs. unifying experience?

She had planned to begin her lecture on the poetics of motherhood with the first paragraph of Adrienne Rich's essential (one cannot say seminal) book *Of Woman Born*.

All human life on the planet is born of woman. The one unifying, incontrovertible experience shared by all women and men is that months-long

1. This punctuation mark was invented by Becca Klaver. I first learned of it through Arielle Greenberg.

period we spent unfolding inside a woman's body. Because young humans remain dependent upon nurture for a much longer period than other mammals, and because of the division of labor long established in human groups, where women not only bear and suckle but are assigned almost total responsibility for children, most of us first know both love and disappointment, power and tenderness, in the person of a woman.

She had been planning to talk about Rich's use of the word "unifying," the fact that Rich had not written "universal." Motherhood, she was planning to say, is not universal, and one of the great things that motherhood accomplishes, if one is paying attention and speaking with a mothermind and mothervoice, is the way in which motherhood subverts the entire concept of universality. The pregnant body, for example, is not a machine and not a broken machine and not a deviant variation of the male form. But how could she even write "the pregnant body" as if that meant any one thing? How could she talk about the unifying experience of motherhood when her experience of it and the institution of it was so vastly different for her and for other mothers?[2]

Rich: "In the division of labor according to gender, the makers and sayers of culture, the namers, have been the sons of the mothers. There is much to suggest that the male mind has always been haunted by the force of the idea of *dependence on a woman for life itself*, the son's constant effort to assimilate, compensate for, or deny the fact that he is 'of woman born.'"

Yes, she felt certain that she must say something. That she must write a lecture about the patriarchy, about what it meant for women and par-

2. Adrienne Rich was grievously and explicitly trans-exclusionary in her later writing, especially in her work on and support of *The Transsexual Empire*.

ticularly for mothers to live and make art centuries into this division of labor. But what about the division of labor as it was unequally distributed (enforced) along the color line? OK, yes, "the male mind." But what about the white, colonial mind? What about the most basic, critical, essential, foundational question of autonomy over one's body and definition of self and the unequal access human beings had had to that autonomy? What about the history of enslavement, violence, and captivity —did that invalidate any meaningful investigation of what might possibly be called a poetics of motherhood?

Brenda Hillman:

A new set of *betweennesses* happened in language as her body came and went through time and distance. Individual words fell apart. Colors became letters. Yellow was plural, was daughters of yellow. Red was too much. Words like "see" "you" "soon" grated themselves into the air. A poetic method, which had heretofore been based on waiting for insight, suddenly had to accommodate process, an indeterminate physics, a philosophy that combined spiritual searching with detached looking. In this procedure of baffled decenteredness, my daughter and I shared a method of *across*.

Mothermind? Mothervoice? Betweennesses? A method of across? She imagined her male editor in the audience cringing. Maybe she should just go back to one of the other lectures, maybe the one about photography, where she talked about Dorothea Lange, Robert Frank, Sally Mann and how being influenced by photography and photographers had led to her photopoetics and her obsession with authenticity, sentimentality, documentary poetics, and the ethics of representation? Yes, she should give any of those other lectures for which she had the armor of a long bibliography of sources. Not armor, but at least a very well-padded and supportive nursing bra. But this?! This hysterical, motherly, terribly interruptible and associational style of inquiry—surely everyone would see that she was leaking—visibly, bodily—that she was unscholarly, intellectually naked, and unworthy in front of the slightest audience.

She had two weeks left, but her husband's grandfather had died and her husband had learned from her mother's death that it was important to show up for people, because some people had not shown up for her, and look how that turned out. So they had flown to Los Angeles with the children and eaten pastrami and cookies and all the things that made her feel tremendously unwell. They had driven on the perilous highways in a rented minivan with the children cursing and shouting and crying, and the husband had given a eulogy in which he said his grandfather had managed during his long life of passionate, hard work and seventy-two years of marriage to compartmentalize his work and make his family feel like there was nowhere he would rather be. She had held her crying son and had cried. She had cried thinking about how no one would describe her this way or her husband this way. They were doing a shit job compartmentalizing. She was trying and trying to be present, but she was not present. She was always not writing the lecture on the poetics of motherhood.

She had thirteen days. She had twelve days. Ten days. Triage.

On her way to work she listened to a podcast about triage, about what happened at Memorial Baptist during Hurricane Katrina and how it had come to pass—as the waters rose and the medical staff was cut off from the outside world, as the news (erroneously) reported that help was not on the way, that there was looting and rioting, as the hospital was overflowing with sewage, backup generators failing or failed, as they had "put down" their pets—that the nurses gave the most critical and hardest-to-transport patients lethal doses of morphine less than an hour before the helicopters arrived.

Her son said, "It's really bad timing that you've been away so much." Her other son said, "I hate you and I am never talking to you again." Her other son said, "Can you please just once read me a book that is not so scary and upsetting?" She had been reading him *The Watsons Go to Birmingham—1963* and had just read Christopher Paul Curtis's description of nine-year-old Kenny's experience of the 16th Street Baptist Church bombing. She lay in bed with her youngest son and held him. She could not think of a single book that was not scary and thought about the email she'd gotten from a friend that had said, "I'm so sick of white parents protecting their white kids from everything. It has to stop."

Her son was scared of Trump. Her other sons had told their little brother that Trump might win. They had told him that if Trump won it meant the end of democracy. They told him men were bad. They told him white people were bad. They told him racism and misogyny and xenophobia were bad. They defined these terms for him. Her son, nine years old, had perfected an uncanny imitation of Trump that was freaky and disturbing and delighted everyone who listened to him and resulted in him walking around saying, "Nasty woman, such a nasty woman," under his breath whenever he was not singing the lyrics to *Hamilton* or playing *FIFA* or updating his YouTube channel with soccer freestyling moves that he and his best friend performed while James (her former student and a former collegiate-level goalkeeper who sometimes babysat for her son) filmed on his phone.

She had not taught her sons to cook. She had not taught them to do laundry. She had not taught them to clean. She had taught them that racism was bad. She had taught them misogyny and homophobia and xenophobia and Islamophobia were bad. One of them hated her, but none of them hated women. She had no idea if she was living her life in right relation to anything, if she was protecting them too much or not enough.

When trying to describe how she felt, she kept making and erasing metaphors. She wrote, "It was hard to know if the helicopters were coming," but Isaac kindly told her over and over again that she should not employ such metaphors. She knew it was offensive to use the real-life tragedies of others—others who were less fortunate, less free, less powerful than she—to describe her own powerlessness, her worry, her fragmentation, her feeling that she was the dog in the box shocked over and over without rhyme or reason that she had learned about in Intro Psych. And still she did it: used metaphor, engaged in imaginative identification, wrote offensive poems, and continued to think about motherhood as if that were a meaningful category. "Are you trying to get us to feel sorry for privileged white women?" her son had asked in the Q and A after her lecture on confessional poetry.

"He will not win," she said, when her sons spoke to her in numbers. They said, "He might win, he could win." They were nearly math geniuses, these boys, and they said something that was mostly numbers and then the word "margins" and said he was likely to win. But she was the mother and believed in the goodness of humankind and in other mothers. She said, "It is very important to distinguish between beliefs and worries. You are *worried* he will win, but no one *believes* he will win. He will not win." "Why not?" they said. There were trying not to mansplain to her, but they were reading the numbers and watching the news. They were not sleeping or doing homework. They were exhaustedly, despairingly, constantly refreshing their devices. She said, "I will give you each $500 if he wins. I am that sure he will not win." She said, "It should be enough to be disqualified for being a racist, homophobic bigot, but it's not. That's the sad, sad truth. But you can't get up and say those things about women and have women vote for you. No woman will vote for him. And enough men who care about women will not vote for him. It's in the bag. We will have our first mother president, you'll see. And yes," she said, "it *will* matter."

That was her fucking poetics, right there, her poetics of motherhood.

She had told the students: "Write down as many associations as you have with the word 'mother.' Circle the things that most surprised you. Put a star next to the ones that spark something for you."

A book said: The Beats rejected family and wanted more authenticity and less responsibility.

Jane Smiley wrote: "Successful motherhood is a unique form of responsibility-taking, rooted in an understanding of competing demands, compromise, nurture, making the best of things, weighing often competing limitations, in order to arrive at a realistic mode of survival."

A book said: The family oppressed men and women differently.

A book said: To achieve liberation, women must be freed from the burden of producing children in their bodies, a burden that limits, distorts, and degrades women. Firestone proposes extrauterine gestation in test tubes as a liberationist strategy. Only then, she argues, will the biological family cease to define women's lives.

She had written, "Notley and Mayer are writing about consciousness," on a little piece of paper that was somewhere in her apartment.

She wrote: "The 1970s saw a re-endorsement of motherhood in part because the counterculture offered 'the politics of everyday life as its only program' and because white feminists were trying to bring women together as a movement and motherhood had always been a central concern of black feminists. Also, reconceiving motherhood as a potentially unifying force for feminism was foundational for ecofeminism and feminist peace activist theory. —Source?"

"The poetics of everyday life," she wrote, "but not Frank O'Hara or James Schuyler or Allen Ginsberg."

Over the summer, she had spoken to her editor and had told him she wanted to write a new lecture, a lecture on the poetics of motherhood. He had not said no. He had not said yes. That was not their way with one another. He had said, "Haven't you already written about that?" Or he might have said something else, but that is what she heard. She had misheard him before. Had misheard him and other important men and had often had to apologize for mishearing them. She was frequently apologizing for possibly mishearing the things that important men were saying to her.

It was ten days. It was eight days. She was staying up until two or three in the morning writing or actively trying not to write the lecture and having to get up at six to make breakfast. Her goal was to be kind to the children and to the husband before they left for school. She was failing. She was tired and angry, and the election was a week away.

All my poems are the poetics of motherhood, she thought. Maybe she could just read the poem about her second son's birth, a poem that split her, a poem that redefined her poetics and her relationship to language.

She wrote: "When white women fought for abortion rights they were mostly tone-deaf to how this sounded to black women who had endured forced sterilization, often without their knowledge. What does this have to do with the poetics of motherhood?"

"The poetics of motherhood is always what is knowable and unknowable," she wrote on her phone, in the dark, when she was wide awake, trying not to write her lecture because really it was not safe, not safe at all, to be so tired and have to drive her son to soccer in the morning. She tried listening to a podcast instead of making notes on her phone. On the podcast, Marina Abramović said, "If you make the bread in a bakery, you're a baker. If you make the bread in a gallery, you're an artist."

A book said: The decontextualizing of motherhood was a strategy to neutralize the tensions between lesbians and heterosexual women in the movement.

Fuck me, she thought. Did she have to write about the relationship between the anti-porn movement and feminism in order to write about the poetics of motherhood?

Her feminist husband had no idea that she was writing and not writing her lecture on the poetics of motherhood night after night. Her feminist husband did not want her to write another lecture. He did not mind the very confessional poems she had written about their family, about herself, about him, but he did not like her lecture voice. Her feminist husband did not know she was up almost all night every night, beginning on the night of the day that she and James had decided once and for all not to write the lecture on the poetics of motherhood. Her feminist husband did not know this because they were not sleeping in the same room and had not been for many months.

Triage, she thought.

The writing of Mayer, Notley, Ostriker, Olds, and and and . . . must be seen in the context of what other feminists were doing from 1976–1980, which was writing about daily experience, consciously making motherhood visible, analyzing lived experience in ways that were central to feminist theory, central to a desire for connectedness and authenticity. She would have written a sentence just like that if she were writing her lecture on the poetics of motherhood.

Tillie Olsen: "Without intention of or pretension to literary scholarship, I have had special need to learn all I could of this over the years, myself so nearly remaining mute and having to let writing die over and over again in me."

Tillie Olsen: "More than in any other human relationship, overwhelmingly more, motherhood means being instantly interruptible, responsive, responsible."

Tillie Olsen: "What possible difference, you may ask, does it make to literature whether or not a woman writer remains childless—free choice or not—especially in view of the marvels these childless women have created.

Might there not have been other marvels as well, or other dimensions to these marvels? Might there not have been present profound aspects and understandings of human life as yet largely absent in literature?"

Alice Notley: "When I began *Disobedience*, I wanted to see if I could combine all of the elements of my previous work into one work—that is, autobiography as daily commentary and daily involvement in politics (I mean politics by virtue of one's being oneself, and part of the world), along with fictional narrative, with characters, and fantasy and dream."

She had a dream, the night before the election, that she was handling shit. It was a long and vivid dream. She was trying to hold the shit but it was slipping and falling and getting everywhere.

Alice Notley: "But yes, my interest in the long poem also has to do with taking it away from men, though . . . I also feel the pressure of a feminized tradition."

From Notley's poem "Dear Dark Continent":

doing of everything experience is thought of

but I've ostensibly chosen
                    my, a, *family*
so early! so early! (as is done always
as it would seem always) I'm a two
now three irrevocably
                    I'm wife I'm mother I'm
myself and him and I'm myself and him and him

But isn't it only I in the real
whole long universe? Alone to be
in whole long universe?

But I and this he (and he) makes ghosts of
I and all the *hes* there would be, won't be

because by now I am he, we are I, I am we.

Maybe she could write it on the plane, but how could she pack all the necessary books? Did she even have time to find the notes in the apartment on little pieces of paper, and what if she had dreamed the notes instead of having written them in real life?

Toi Derricotte in *Natural Birth*:

i

grew deep
in me
like fist and i

grew deep
in me
like death
    and i
grew deep
in me
like hiding in the sea and
i was
over me
like
sun and i
was under
me
like sky and i
could look
into myself
like one
dark eye.
. . . .

    he is not i
    i am not him
    he is not i

Triage, she thought. She should stop speaking. She should stop writing. She should shut the fuck up. She should not write a lecture on the poetics of motherhood. She should just make a quilt of quotes from the mother-poets who had made her who she was. But she did not have time to sew the squares and would leave too many out—too many mothers, too many motherwords. The poetics of motherhood would have to include every word written by every mother-poet (at least since 1976) in the world, and not even Bernadette Mayer would be able to accomplish such a feat.

Ostriker:

> We are struggling against amnesia and denial. Good motherhood, in our culture, is selfless, cheerful, and deodorized. It does not include resentment, anger, violence, alienation, disappointment, grief, fear, exhaustion —or erotic pleasure. It is ahistorical and apolitical.

Rich: "We know more about the air we breathe, the seas we travel, than about the nature and meaning of motherhood."

She was lying awake in her bedroom that she now slept in alone listening to seventeen-year-old son sob as the results came in. She was not looking her sons in the eye; how could she? She was crying on the subway on the way to teach, watching the other white women on the NYC subway crying and loving them and hating them. She was crying through her undergraduate workshop, crying her white woman, white fragility tears as her female undergraduates cried, occasionally running from the room to take calls from their mothers, one sobbing and speaking in Farsi, a black student refusing to speak or take out a pen—she was trying to stop crying and could not stop crying and could not stop apologizing.

People were tweeting poems, and people of color were saying her shock and despair were offensive in that they were a mark of her privilege and whiteness, that she had failed to recognize that things had always been this bad for marginalized people and for people of color. People were tweeting facts and maps, and there was no way to look away from what she had never imagined: the majority of white women had not voted for a first woman president, for a first mother president, they had instead voted for a racist, misogynist, anti-intellectual, rapist lunatic. She felt a precipitous hatred for white women, of which she was one. She felt hatred for white people, of which she was one. She felt hatred particularly but not only for cis white men, of which her husband and beautiful sons—how could she ever untangle this hatred of hatred with anything other than hatred? How had she been so mistaken as to believe women would never vote for him, that men who loved women would never vote for him? Some insidious disgust for all women (of which she was one) and the sick white male obsession to protect white women (of which she was one)—the imagined vulnerability of white women and the white supremacist fixation surrounding the imperiled chastity of white women—and white supremacy which was perniciously entrenched in ways her whiteness had made it hard to perceive—

It was two days, it was one day. It was the day. It was the next day. It was no day. It was night. It was not the same night and nights she had nursed the first the second the third or the night nights she had lost the baby between her second and third, the night nights of bleeding and waiting. It was not the night nights she had lain in bed with the husband or the night nights she had stayed awake writing or worrying or the night the doctors in Taiwan had turned off the heart-lung machine, and she had listened to the sound of the change of the sound of the room without the heart-lung machine that had been forcing the blood and oxygen into and through her mother's body and then a long, single sound and no sound. It was not the night of her mother's death. It was not the night nights of her babies' first cries. It was not the night nights she had con-ceived new life, but it *was* that night, *is* that night, all those nights, for the poetics of motherhood (if there is one, and she believed there was) began before recorded time and is larger than our human understanding of time. The poetics of motherhood may be the birth of what we call "a theory of mind," intersubjectivity, empathy. The poetics of motherhood may very well be what makes us human—not our use of tools, not walking on two legs, not the ability to use language—it is the song of being born, of caring for another above oneself, of needing help, of a lost goddess, of the long, long night of love and pain.

AUTHOR'S NOTE

At the end of September 2012, I was invited to write three original lectures that I would deliver in at least three locations in the spring of 2016. I agreed. Four months later my mother died while we were in the middle of a fight about my book, *MOTHERs*. I published *MOTHERs*, but believed I would never write again. More specifically, I knew I would honor my commitment to write the lectures, but I imagined I would never write poems or memoir again. So, from 2014 to 2016 I read, researched, thought about, wrote, and rewrote five lectures, and from December 2015 to November 2016 (with a gap from May to October) I went on a ten-state tour delivering versions of the lectures or essays or talks in this book.

During the gap in my lecture tour, I started *Commonplace*, a long-form conversation podcast with poets and artists, partly as a way of reviving my two favorite parts of the lecture tour: the question and answer sessions at the end of each lecture and the intimate, intense conversations I'd had with local poets and docents while I was traveling. Starting my podcast was also, I realize in retrospect, a way to counteract the emotional whiplash I felt each time I returned home after giving a lecture. One day I'd be in a dimly lit restaurant in Tucson or Pittsburgh, post-lecture, discussing marriage, teaching, social justice, God, exercise, sex, cooking, and poetry. I'd return home after speaking to an audience of people who seemed to think I had something valuable to say to: "where are my boots?!" and "I don't want to do my homework!!" That's part of being a mom, of course, and being a mom can be intellectually stimulating and fascinating, particularly with my kids, but it was a rough transition. Trump's election accelerated my older sons' struggles with mental illness, and my marriage was slowly eroding my sense of self. My husband didn't like my lectures or my "lecture voice," and there were too many nights when he could barely tolerate the fifteen minutes of time with me prescribed by our couples therapist. To go from feeling interesting and interested to feeling boring, long-winded, pedantic, and old was devastating. I began to realize that in addition to starting *Commonplace* as a way of compelling extraordinary living artists to sit down and talk to me, I'd also created a measurable way (downloads) to gauge whether people were interested, whether anyone was listening.

The talks in this book are organized in the order in which I wrote them, although each lecture changed substantially in response to editorial feedback from readers and the question and answer sessions that followed each lecture. The last lecture—which I was meant to deliver on November 11, 2016 in Portland, Oregon—I only gave once. Literary Arts, along with most of downtown Portland, was shut down as people passionately protested the election of Donald Trump. I read "Why She Could Not Write a Lecture on the Poetics of Motherhood" a few days later in Berkeley, CA. That was the last official gig of my lectureship but not the end of working on the lectures and making (and resisting making) them into a book. I would continue to work on them in intensive, intermittent bursts for five more years.

Meanwhile, all this time, I was teaching. I'd always had an antiauthoritarian streak, but my commitment to nonhierarchical teaching solidified when I trained to become a labor doula and encountered a completely different kind of education than I'd experienced at Yale and the Iowa Writer's Workshop. I practiced supporting people without trying to fix them or their challenges. I encountered the power of trying to stay in the present. When I'd come home from the lectures to my family and students and feel the urge to assume an expert/authoritarian approach in the classroom (or in writing the next lecture), I would remind myself that I didn't believe in this type of teaching (or writing) anymore. Tearing down the parts of myself that could have given me the confidence to deliver traditional lectures was painful, but I knew it was the right direction for me to go in as a mother, educator, and human being.

Slowly, sheepishly, I began writing poems—or prose that felt like poems, or lectures with line breaks—while I was supposed to be working on the lectures. Some of these prosems were experiments in confessionality. Some of them (I realized later) were exercises in breaking the ethical guidelines I was writing about in the lectures. These new pieces, along with older genre-nonconforming pieces, came together in *Sound-Machine* (Wave, 2019). I imagined that the lecture book and *SoundMachine* would be published around the same time and would be read as companion pieces with overlapping concerns, but as I turned my attention to *SoundMachine* (both the book and an accompanying immersive audio project), it became more and more difficult to finish the lecture book.

In January 2018 I spent twenty-eight bitterly cold and gloriously solitary days at MacDowell expanding the lectures by elaborating, thinking, and writing about what it meant to turn lectures into essays. Poet and scholar Isaac Ginsberg Miller, a former student of mine, accompanied me on this leg of the journey. By phone and over email, Isaac challenged me to think more carefully and complexly. He listened. He was interested. He wanted me to write more and say more. He became the stead-fast interlocutor I needed to keep going.

The essays or talks that appear in this book are a result of this process, but the version I finished at MacDowell also contained lectures that don't appear here. My lecture on photography: "Photopoetics: One Poet's Obsession with Authenticity, Sentimentality, Activism, and the Ethics of Representation," which I delivered at Yale in 2016, turned into an eighty-plus page memoir, with photographs by my favorite photographers and some of my own. My lecture "She Who Shall Not Be Named or *if you don't have anything nice to say why are you still talking?*" (which I read aloud only once for an audience of three at my friend Deirdre's apartment) catalogued everything I'd written that had hurt people or gotten me into trouble. At MacDowell, I expanded "She Who Shall Not Be Named" to include my mother's final emails to me and mine to her as well as a long consideration of the potential violence of poetry, prose, and story. The MacDowell version of *The Poetics of Wrongness* contained interstitial material—poems, mini-essays, an interview of me by poet Christine Larusso (former student and *Commonplace* producer), as well as a list of questions from people who had been fundamental to me in writing the book: Isaac Ginsberg Miller, Jeremy Bendik-Keymer, Tom Shakow, Joy Katz, Erika Meitner, Erin Murray Marra, David Trinidad, Colin Beckett, Matthew Zapruder, Daniel Shiffman, Wayne Koestenbaum, Charlie Wright, Katy Lederer, Josh Goren, Nicholas Fuenzalida, Laurel Snyder, Arielle Greenberg, my father, and Heidi Broadhead.

After a year or so of revising this expanded version of the lectures but feeling like something wasn't right, my new editor, Heidi Broadhead, suggested we try going back to the expanded four core lectures and take out the other material. It was discouraging, at first, to prune the sprawling, maximalist tome, but the MacDowell version had become a book about how I'd come to write a book of lectures and how I'd come to realize that my lectures were thinly-veiled attempts at explaining myself to my (dead) mother. The lectures themselves were lost within my thinking about the process.

One central concern in *SoundMachine* and in these lectures is the relationship between time and art: how to be in the present and how to make visible the fact that no writing exists outside of its moment, outside of the lived personal history of the author, the weather, who is in power politically. The fewer-but-expanded lectures made for a clearer, more honest (and better!) book, but I hated the idea of publishing them without acknowledging how much has happened since I'd started the project. I felt compelled to describe my current circumstances, but every time I wrote something, my current circumstances had changed.

When I started these lectures my boys were fifteen, fourteen, and seven. "Today" they are twenty-two, twenty, and fourteen—different people, almost. The older boys struggled mightily during those years—graduated high school, went to college or took a gap year, took leaves, went back to college, became men. My youngest is now a teenager.

I've changed, too. On the fifth anniversary of my mother's death, I performed an untying ritual to free myself from any possible curses—imagined, real, or self-imposed. A month later, I ended up in urgent care, dizzy, weak and dangerously anemic. The months that followed are a blur. My oldest son and I traveled to Taiwan to meet the people who were with my mother when she died, and to see the place she loved so much. From Taiwan, we traveled to Japan and met up with my husband and other sons for what would be our last trip as a family. Despite many mainstream and allopathic treatments, I barely made it home. I was bleeding heavily from uterine fibroids and ended up with an emergency hysterectomy two months later. Recurring panic attacks and a depressive episode followed. It was not an easy time.

I wrote what was to be a long ending to this book, about my trip to Taiwan, about stories, anemia, and about endings themselves. Heidi helped me see that this ending was possibly the beginning of a new piece of writing but not the right ending to the collection of lectures. Time passed. In early March 2020, a few days before New York City shut down from COVID-19, I flew to Maine and told my husband I was done trying to improve our marriage. I lived in lockdown with my future ex-husband and our three sons for three months while initiating separation and divorce proceedings. The lecture book was pretty low on my list of priorities, especially because every time I looked at it, I thought, "I have to write a different ending; this book is obviously all about the end of my marriage!" And how could I not write about COVID? And how could I not write about the Trump years?

Time passed. COVID time. I lived in Maine, in a house I bought with money I'd inherited from my mother. I cooked three meals a day for five people. I got a puppy. I taught remotely. I walked on the same beach every day in every season. I started a garden. I put on very loud music and sobbed and danced in my bedroom. Every minute the present became the past. And every time I returned to the lectures, I had new things to add or take out. I added and took out paragraphs. I went back and gathered previously published writing from the past ten years, short essays and talks in which I had explored some of the topics that became central questions of my lectures. I liked the way multiple considerations of the same subjects subverted the authority of the final versions of the lectures in this book, and decided to add some of them (see appendix), but I still felt uneasy. It felt like I'd never be able to let these lectures out into the world in written form.

For example, "now," in my middle age—post-hysterectomy, post-marriage—I have more complicated and nuanced ideas about gender. Actually, I don't have more ideas—I have more questions! More curiosity. More awe. But that didn't make it into the book. Instead, in these lectures, I'm often talking about cis womanhood but not specifying cis womanhood, and not considering the experiences of trans women. I don't push back on Adrienne Rich's history of transphobia. I say things about feminisms that imply I believe in a gender binary, but that's not my personal experience or my intellectual belief anymore.

Also, when Trump was elected, it raised another kind of wrongness that was *not* the kind of wrongness I was talking about embracing. I hadn't believed that Trump could happen. I didn't understand that Trump—not as a person, but as a system—had already happened and had been happening. I feel clearer now about the origin of my shock at Trump. Poet, editor, and *Commonplace* producer Valentine Conaty became an unflinching interlocutor and helped me clarify several essential points in the lectures that helped the expansion I did in 2018. Valentine also helped me accept that I would not be able to fully update these lectures unless I were to start over again and write entirely new lectures. So my reaction to Trump's election and the anti-racism work I've done since are not explicitly in this book, either.

I have such mixed feelings about making claims. I have mixed feelings about the lectures written down like this, without an introduction tailored to each audience, with one immutable, unchangeable ending, particularly at a time when everything in my personal life (and body) is changing radically and the entire planet feels submerged in uncertainty. Publication feels so final and limiting. I want the book to be my *best* thinking, my *final* thinking, of course, but that's not what the book is about, and as soon as I get into that mindset, I've made the book into an idol. I don't want to seem a fool, don't want to seem inconsiderate or a shoddy thinker, but on my more lucid days I feel closer to being comfortable with what is, as opposed to imposing (or seeking) some kind of purity, perfection, or ideal form.

A few months ago, my son Abram took me to the Mount Sinai emergency room because I was experiencing severe abdominal pain. Because of COVID, they wouldn't let Abram in. I refused morphine, wanting to stay alert without anyone else to advocate for me. The pain was immense but somehow not frightening. Immersed in pain, I experienced a state of acute awareness and presentness—aliveness—that I had not felt before except when in labor. After twelve hours of waiting, three witchy gynecologic oncologists appeared beside my gurney and gave me a troubling report. Later that week, two other doctors confirmed I would need surgery to determine if the large mass on my right ovary was cancerous. I wouldn't know until I woke up from surgery if I had cancer or even what kind of surgery they'd done.

What followed were three weeks of waiting and planning. It was a time of great clarity. Other than my children, closest friends and a few members of my family, I cared about very little. I moved out of the apartment I'd lived in for twenty-three years. It was the apartment where I'd raised all my sons and birthed my youngest, where I'd wept my apology into the phone to my unconscious mother as the doctors turned off the heart-lung machine, where I'd cooked for and laughed with and fought with my husband, where I'd read hundreds of books to my children and to myself, where I'd written and revised the lectures and ten other books. Clear-eyed, I signed the divorce papers, changed my will and health proxy, put my friend Joan in charge of everything that mattered most, and moved to Washington Heights, a neighborhood I'd never spent time in but loved immediately. My priorities were unambiguous. And I was surprised to find that finishing this book was one of those priorities. I asked Isaac to record a Zoom conversation with me. I hadn't written a poem, essay, or anything substantial for over two years, and I'd come to suspect that my preferred form of language-driven art is, above all, conversation. I talked to Isaac about what I wanted to say at the end of this book and why I was having so much trouble writing what I wanted to say in any form. A transcript was made, and I tried to edit the transcript—just my answers—into something readable that still had the feeling of conversation or at least of spoken language.

"I never say this to you," poet and young adult author Laurel Snyder said to me on the phone after she read the edited transcript of that conversation, "but this isn't working." We talked for a long time. She reminded me that a transcript of a conversation is not a conversation, an edited transcript is not a lecture and not an essay, a lecture is not an essay, and an essay read aloud is not a lecture.

"But the present keeps changing!" I complained. "I want some sort of way to put the lectures in context, to explain—"

"It *is* weird," she said, "to publish a book of lectures, lectures that have changed so many times and that were meant for a particular audience on a particular day."

"I need a removable, updatable ending to the book," I said.

"Then end with a URL that you update from time to time. It can be an invitation to the audience to ask questions and keep the conversation going," she said, "Or don't. Or write a poem, because that's what your poems do. Maybe a poem is the closest thing you can get to a conversation on the page."

NOVEMBER 2021

APPENDIX

SELECTED PROSE (2010–2020)

TERRIBLY SENTIMENTAL

169

AN ANATOMY OF THE LONG POEM

175

A HOMESPUN OF QUESTIONS PULLED OVER A LOOM OF
GENDER AND RACE WITH THE VOICES OF ANCESTRAL
(MOSTLY LIVING) WOMEN SPEAKING IN THE LACUNAE

185

CONFESSIONALOGRAPHY: A GNAT
(GROSSLY NONACADEMIC TALK) ON "I" IN POETRY

195

RACHEL ZUCKER ON HER BOOK SOUNDMACHINE

205

TERRIBLY SENTIMENTAL

The tangle: sentiment, feeling, narrative, storymaking, storytelling, autobiography, confession, sentimentality, revelation, manipulation, relationship with audience, translation of experience, birth.

1. First of all, I wanted to write experience. Wanted to make a writing that would enact experience, not write "about" things, which was very much out of vogue when I studied at Iowa under Jorie Graham. I believed poetry was better than prose in that poems could enact rather than recount experience, and while I believed in the power of stories, I felt that storymaking always involved a lie but that poems could be true.

2. My first book, *Eating in the Underworld*, is a series of poems told through the narrative arc of the myth of Persephone. The poems are about being the daughter of a powerful mother, falling in love, being pulled into darkness, craving power. They are also about the death of my best friend's boyfriend who died, in bed with her, when they were both nineteen and at the University of Wisconsin. Almost no one knows this specific personal allusion because I speak "through" (Persephone) and autobiography is subsumed or strained through or refracted.

3. In 2001, as I was finishing writing my second book, *The Last Clear Narrative*, my friend Arielle Greenberg asked me to send her a poem for

How2, an online feminist journal. I knew right away that I wanted to send a birth poem. I was trying, in *The Last Clear Narrative*, to write my experiences in ways that were personal but NOT sentimental. This was an overt goal. I felt that sentimentality was a way of lying and that I had not been told the truth about motherhood, childbirth, being a woman, being an individual, being a daughter . . . basically anything. I wanted to write experience in a way that felt accurate; I viewed accuracy as the antithesis of sentimentality. I'd never seen an "accurate" poem about birth. I'd written about the birth but the poem was too clean and sanitized (unlike birth!) and so I went back and back, trying to get at the truth of that experience, which was traumatic and non-linear and fragmented and broken open. I wasn't trying to write an "experimental" poem because it was in fashion. I needed to write a broken poem because that's what that birth was for me—self-immolating, self-doubling, terrifying, and profoundly unsentimental.

Writing that poem made the second book clear to me—I'd been trying to describe how marriage and children had broken me physically and upended my understanding of narrative. I was trying to write a poetry that was accurate because to do otherwise was to participate in a culture that tried (tries) to silence women and women's experiences.

4. My third book, *The Bad Wife Handbook* is, in part, a defense of my second book and an experiment with extreme directness. I tried to be more and more direct while trying to still be accurate—not sentimental. The book is about desire, lust, motherlove, the conflict between the "I" and the family. Also, I had started writing about things as a kind of rebellion and also because the alternative was to actually do things and that would have meant leaving my husband and children. Still not sen-

timental—never sentimental—but yes, steeped in sentiment in the sense of having opinions ("my sentiment exactly") and feelings (emotional sense) and certainly in the sense of "from the senses" in that all my knowledge and experience came from my senses. I am a feeling being and this makes me human.

5. Digression: I have a student who was writing these language driven poems that were smart and evocative but not "meaningful" and didn't move me. I made my students write about the thing they were most afraid to write and she wrote this very spare, narrative poem. She read the poem and we all just sat there in silence because it was so different from her other poems. She said, "I've never written about my father's death—he died during the night when I was eight years old. I've never written about it even though my whole life changed then. I just figured it was too sentimental. Is it? Is it terribly sentimental?" I wrote the phrase "terribly sentimental" in my notebook as I formulated a response. I didn't want to praise her too much for fear of sounding like I only liked narrative poetry (I don't), but it was a terrific poem. Also I was shocked that she'd never written about this pivotal event before. It's not like she had this experience and decided to become an accountant and repress all emotions (of course not all accountants repress their emotions). But, seriously, this is a POET. She's in a graduate MFA program in POETRY. And she'd never written about this before? Something seems terribly wrong with this.

6. As I get older, I become more and more interested in what poetry can do. And not just in what poetry is. For example, when Arielle (the poet who pushed me to write the defining poem about my son's birth) gave

birth to a stillborn baby three years ago, someone sent her a Mary Oliver poem that became very dear to her. I feel ashamed at how I'd dismissed Oliver as a "populist" poet, the deep sigh I'd take when a student wanted me to teach Oliver instead of someone I considered more "serious." That Oliver's poem comforted Arielle, even a little, is worth so much to me now.

7. I have less and less patience with poems that don't in some way engage human emotion. Poems in which I do not feel the presence of a feeling (as well as thinking) human being. This preference is, I think, gendered. I hear my students talk about their fear of sentiment (they seem as afraid of sentiment as of sentimentality or do they just not distinguish between the two?) and I can't figure out where this is coming from. I used to be afraid of writing poetry that sounds like the kind of expression reserved for twelve-step program check-ins, but now I think I prefer that to the mechanistic poetry that wants to be person-less. Is this about age? Gender again?

8. One could argue that my fourth book, *Museum of Accidents*, is all and only about finding a way to say, sincerely, that I love my husband. To speak that most banal of heterosexist clichés and make it really mean something. No, to make me *feel* it. I want a poetry that can say such things. Or, one could argue that *Museum of Accidents* is all and only an attempt to write a poem about my miscarriage—the disappointment I felt, the loss—with sincerity and accuracy. I wanted the reader to feel bludgeoned, to feel sick of me, of my body, of my baby loss, because that's how I felt. The whole culture told me to shut the fuck up about how it felt to lose that baby who wasn't even a baby but only a placenta

and empty sac—just shut up, they said, move on! And I wanted a poetry that would not shut up, and that would not even let the reader "identify" with me or even really feel sorry for me because I didn't want that. I wanted to tell and not tell and to end with the punchlines of jokes. And, even though I'd set out to write an unlovable poem, the poem is highly sentimental. I am writing *about* things. I am revealed as a person who is "excessively prone to feeling" and as a person who wants to make others feel things too.

9. This also has to do with birth. Now that I've given birth three times and been to the births of friends and clients, what none of the books or women or stories ever made clear (were they lying? was I not ready to believe?) is that birth is beautiful and spiritual and also totally mundane and shitty (literally). It is hard work—the lowest and highest—and that's what I'm interested in writing. Not about birth per se but the realness of experience, the permission to write with shame and honesty and humor and ambivalence. Arielle and I cowrote a book called *Home/Birth: A Poemic* and had to do a round of midnight-hour proofreading last week when the editor admitted to us that she hadn't done a great job proofreading because when she reads the manuscript she bursts into tears. I'm proud of that. For having written something about birth that makes a woman who has not given birth cry, for writing a book that makes anyone cry. Sentiment and sentimental. Aboutness.

10. For a long time, if someone asked me what my favorite poem was, I'd answer "A Baby is Born out of a White Owl's Forehead, 1972" by Alice Notley. I loved Notley's poem for the last line "but first, for two years, there's no me here," which seemed like the most accurate description

possible of what it felt like for me in the first two years after my second son was born. I felt so grateful that I had these lines. They meant so much to me. The "sentiment" was true and kept me afloat when I felt alone and lied to. Recently (years later), I went back to Notley's poem when writing an essay (which has turned into a book about my mother and Notley and Graham and stories versus poems and memory), and I saw, underlined in my own hand, these lines I hadn't remembered at all: "Of two poems one sentimental and one not / I choose both" and I started to cry because that's everything I've tried to do in my poetry in the past fifteen years.

2010

AN ANATOMY OF
THE LONG POEM

Consider, for example, "Lying in a Hammock at William Duffy's Farm in Pine Island, Minnesota," by James Wright, and "A Man Meets a Woman in the Street," by Randall Jarrell. In Wright's poem, the speaker, lying in a hammock, sees a butterfly on the trunk of a tree. He notices cowbells in the distance and horse droppings in an adjacent field. A chicken hawk flies over, evening approaches, and the speaker says, mysteriously, "I have wasted my life."

In Jarrell's poem, the speaker walks behind a beautiful blond-haired woman. He describes the woman and then thinks about Konrad Lorenz, Richard Strauss, Marcel Proust, Greta Garbo, his early morning walk, the difference between birds and human beings, the nature of human relationships. The speaker catches up to the woman, who turns out to be his wife. He touches her, kisses her, walks through the sunlit park with her, and realizes his worldview is more bird-like than human-like, that really he began the day "with the birds' wish: 'May this day / Be the same day, the day of my life.'"

When one looks at these poems closely, closely enough to see the brush strokes, textures, and colors, the two poems have almost nothing in common. But from a distance, the poems look almost identical: description, bits of narrative, epiphany.

The middle distance interests me. Both speakers are in motion (one in a hammock, the other walking) and apprehending something else in motion (the fluttering butterfly, the woman who is walking). In both poems, the speaker begins in a state of heightened attentiveness and is primarily concerned with discerning subtle differences of color (a bronze butterfly on a black trunk like a "leaf in green shadow" or the woman whose "hair's coarse gold / Is spun from the sunlight that it rides upon"). They are trying to distinguish the particular from the general. Both poets look closely, then pull back. Wright describes the sounds of cowbells moving away in a ravine he cannot see. Jarrell wanders off to the land of memory. Then something brings them back. The evening comes on and envelops Wright; Jarrell touches his wife and stops pretending she's just any woman. In coming into contact with the physical world and his immediate present, each is shocked into an awakening or epiphany of self-knowledge.

I confess: I like Jarrell's poem more than Wright's. Maybe it's as simple as liking the hopeful epiphany rather than the despairing one. Perhaps I'm compelled to ascribe the decidedly male voice of the speaker to my husband and am romanced by the "after all these years my wife is so beautiful to me and I have everything I ever wanted" narrative and terrified by the "I've wasted my life" sentiment.

I think the main reason I prefer Jarrell's poem is its length. Some might find this a fallacious argument, but I submit that the structures/shapes/movements of these poems are nearly identical and that the greatest difference between them lies in the fact that Wright's poem is thirteen lines whereas Jarrell's poem is ninety-seven lines. It is in the "extraneous" parts of Jarrell's poem, in his digressions and diversions, that I come to know and like Jarrell's speaker, begin to know his mind, feel involved, included, invested (even though I'm not privy to all the references and allusions he makes), so that when Jarrell writes, "Because, after all, it *is* my wife" and "We first helped each other, hurt each other, years ago," my breath catches and my eyes well up.

If two poems are similar but one is longer, is the longer one always better? Of course not. If a poem is poorly written, it will be unpleasant and disappointing, and the longer it goes on, the more the unfortunate reader will suffer. On the other hand, I don't find shortness itself to be a virtue.

There are many short poems I admire and, of course, too many wonderful midlength poems to name that I adore. But I have a special love for a good long poem, and long poems have more in common than just their length.

Long poems are extreme. They're too bold, too ordinary, too self-centered, too expansive, too grand, too banal, too weird, too much. They revel in going too far; they eschew caution and practicality and categorization and even, perhaps, poetry itself, which as a form tends to value the economy of language. Long poems seem almost compelled to subvert (often by assimilating) genre categories. Long poems are anti-tweets though they often contain twitter-like language.

Long poems grapple with narrative. As human beings, we're hardwired to construct stories from the world around us, especially out of anything made of language.

Long poems are especially susceptible to the pull of narrative. I wrote to Alice Notley, a master of the long form, to ask about this. Notley wrote back: "A short poem is composed of the dynamics between each word.

In the poetry of an author like Chaucer there is story, which formally is something like a whale under the surface of the ocean. However, in an author like Homer the form is the story but the form is the line—the length and meter of that line." Narrative is always an important presence in the long poem, either as a "whale under the surface of the ocean" or in the form itself.

Long poems can seem spoken (think of Allen Ginsberg's *Howl* or David Antin's talk poems) or read like a diary (Bernadette Mayer's *Midwinter Day*) or act like a portrait in words of a person, place, or idea (think of William Carlos Williams's *Paterson*, Carolyn Forché's *The Angel of History*, C. D. Wright's *Deepstep Come Shining*), but there's always a voice speaking or a human presence. There's always a story.

If a long poem is going to subvert narrative, it has to be radical. Even then, techniques used in short poems to avoid story-making—relying on images, condensing language, undermining the normal rules of syntax and grammar—often result in a long poem that sounds like an extended story told by a nonnarrative or nonlinear, raw, prophetic, psychedelic voice.

Long poems might not sustain the intense "dynamic between words" that short poems often do, but still find ways to avoid "falling into paragraph," as D. A. Powell, a poet who does not write long poems but loves to read and teach them, says.

Powell: "A long poem that arches from beginning to end with a central consciousness, a directly traceable story, a singular (not necessarily single) purpose, is truly more novel than poem. But it's a novel that relies upon the devices and music of poetry as its motif." The language still has weight and aims to surprise and delight and adhere to itself and to be, on some level, summarizable, irreducible, more than just communication. The line, even when stretched to the limit, is still a line, still a critical measure.

Long poems take time to read. Reading long poems requires a different kind of attention—a longer time commitment but also, realistically, less attention to detail. My mind wanders when reading a long poem, and in this way my reading is more experiential and the experience is almost collaborative, reciprocal. My daydreams and the sensory data of the world around me become ephemerally woven into the long poem as I read so that I feel myself more fully present in the poem even as my mind wanders. My life interrupts the poem, which I can't read in one sustained burst of reconcentration, and the poem interrupts my life as I find I've spent my whole afternoon traveling its landscape.

Long poems are confessional. There is always a human being speaking. There is always the passage of time. There is change, and the reader bears witness to the life or mind of the poet. On the most basic level, all long poems are confessional even if all they confess is how the poet has spent a great deal of time.

Long poems create intimacy. Marriage or a long-term relationship isn't a long one-night stand in which one person never goes home. A long poem isn't just a short poem that the poet forgot to end. Both require and inspire a different mindset, a different pacing, a different way of being, a different kind and level of intimacy with another person and with the self. When reading a good short or midlength poem, I feel a shock of recognition—like catching a stranger's eye on the subway—but this fleeting, intense connection underscores the separation between the poem and me, the otherness of the poet and his world from me and mine. Because of the breaks and points of entry, and simply because of how long I "exist" with and within the poem, I am committed to and invested in a long poem in a way that I can never be with a short poem.

Long poems are "about" something; long poems are about nothing but themselves. D. A. Powell: long poems make "a much bolder claim on the temporal field of poetry, sacrificing individual moments for the sake of broader ideas." There is an inevitable "storyness" or "aboutness" in long poems. Motifs accrue; themes that sound like or are "broader ideas" develop.

Long poems are muralistic or kaleidoscopic rather than overarching; they resist "aboutness." Long poems can sometimes do a better job of salvaging and preserving individual moments than short poems can. In the short poem, individual moments are often used in the service of an idea or to illustrate an argument.

Long poems, on the other hand, tend to resist rhetoric, and I find that what the long poem is most often "about" is itself: the process of extended curiosity, noticing, thinking, and being aware. Individual moments in a long poem are so numerous that they seem to be emblematic only of the writer's consciousness, of the authorial presence, or of the poem-making process. "Life, it seems, explains nothing about itself. In the / Garden now daffodils stand full unfolded and to see them is enough," writes James Schuyler.

Long poems discover themselves. David Trinidad, who writes long and short poems: "I also remember thinking, in the middle of 'A Poem Under the Influence,' that it was like a mural (versus a shorter poem, which is more like a single canvas), so long and wide I couldn't see what was around the corner, or where it would end." Just as the essay is a form in which a writer discovers what she believes, the long poem is a form in which the poet discovers herself and the shape of the poem in the writing.

Long poems allow the poet to change her mind. This is part of the delight of the long poem. "Do I contradict myself? / Very well then I contradict myself, / (I am large, I contain multitudes.)" writes Walt Whitman.

Long poems change the mind. In an interview with Jennifer Dick, Notley said, "What I'm doing is creating—trying to create—a different consciousness . . . And I think this happens for some other people. It actually makes your head different."

Long poems are ambitious. And egotistical. And obnoxious. How can the poet believe others are willing to listen to her go on and on? Who is she to tell the tale of the tribe? Who is she to speak so loudly, for so long, so unceasingly?

Long poems humble the poet. Eleni Sikelianos: "The more I did, the bigger the field appeared, and I knew there was no way I could 'cover' (or manipulate) everything in it. So I had to settle on scratching at this one little spot as diligently (or at least for as long) as I could." The poet writing the long poem is an ant moving crumbs from the majestic picnic, always aware of her own shortcomings and inadequacies. The poet writing a long poem is an artist at work, not a priest offering the "the word" to an illiterate flock. "You shall no longer take things at second or third hand, nor look through the eyes of the dead, nor feed on the spectres in books, / You shall not look through my eyes either, nor take things from me, / You shall listen to all sides and filter them from yourself," writes Whitman.

Long poems are about process and highlight process. Jackson Pollock's paintings are a record of his body's movements and his physical presence in relation to the canvas. The long poem is a record of the poet's mind over time. Not surprisingly, time and progress are often explicit, central themes in the long poem as is the writing process itself. There is a self-consciousness (sometimes an embarrassment) about the project of writing ("I hate fussing with nature and would like the world to be / All weeds . . ." writes Schuyler) but also a compulsion to continue. The long poem is fueled by an unflagging curiosity about the world; "why not leave the world alone?" writes Schuyler in "Hymn to Life," "Then / There would be no books, which is not to be borne."

The poet keeps writing, keeps writing. It is an odd thing to do, a strange way to spend time, but there is the world with its innumerable glories, and what else can a poet do but write?

The attention to process makes the long poem a highly artificial, self-consciously made thing. On the other hand, this embrace of artifice makes the poem feel more honest than poems that aim to impart a feeling while hiding their poemness. Long poems are buildings—sometimes glaringly out of place with the landscape, sometimes meant to blend in almost seamlessly—but never holodecks.

Long poems are sad and full of joy. Death, time, and the changing of the seasons are often the subjects, explicit or implicit, of the long poem. Despite or because of these themes, the long poem is always, on some level, borne of a deep, extended engagement that is also a kind of joy. Many short stories and short poems are rather bleak (sometimes satisfyingly bleak); they feel finished, locked, shut, closed. But the long poem, with its attempts to include everything, is, by its nature, expansive, exuberant, engaged, and overflowing.

Long poems are imperfect. Poets perfect short poems by cutting away everything that doesn't absolutely need to be there. The poem is whittled down or polished the way a diamond cutter carefully facets a stone to allow for the most brilliant capture and dispersion of light. Novellas, short stories, and some novels strive for this kind of just-rightness, the feeling that every single word is necessary, exact. But the long poem has a different mindset.

The long poem embraces and rejects and re-embraces imperfection. Sometimes it does so because it's trying to describe REAL LIFE, and life is imperfect, messy, filled with loose ends. Sometimes the long poem is imperfect because it is a human voice speaking or a human mind thinking, and speech and thought are convoluted, hypocritical, contradictory, and fragmented. Sometimes the long poem is imperfect because striving for perfection is a questionable and problematic pursuit.

The Greek word *telos* and the Hebrew words *tam* or *tamim* are often translated into English as "perfect" or "perfection" but in the original don't mean "flawless." They mean mature, complete, finished. The long poem will never be flawless; it doesn't even want to be. The long poem does reach for *telos* and for *tam*, for completeness, maturity, and the full expression of a process. But it fails in these as well. Despite its love of inclusion, the long poem will always be incomplete. The long poem begins *in medias res*, "mid-affairs," and any ending, no matter how right and true it may feel, is a moment of grief for all the long poem has left out, for the extinguished voice.

Long poems have integrity. Carolyn Forché: "Surely all art is the result of one's having been in danger, of having gone through an experience all the way to the end." But how then do we write about life, being, as we are, always in the middle (not sure how close to the end)? The long poem takes on this task, knowing it will fail, embracing failure and imperfection and contradiction and doubt. In this sense, the long poem has integrity—it has the ability to achieve its own goals and is honest about its making.

Long poems are worth your time. Long poems are similar to shorter poems, to novels, to rants, and to diaries but offer something all their own and tell stories that cannot be told in other forms. Long poems allow the reader to be in the presence (sometimes for a very long time) of boundless curiosity, to witness, as Claudia Rankine wrote, a mind's "cratered understanding of our soul's intimacy within the opportunity that is life."

2010

A HOMESPUN OF QUESTIONS PULLED OVER A LOOM OF GENDER AND RACE WITH THE VOICES OF ANCESTRAL (MOSTLY LIVING) WOMEN SPEAKING IN THE LACUNAE

1. Is a question a feminized form of the statement?

2. What, other than embarrassment—fear of sounding uneducated, unsure, ahistorical, inexpert, unmasculine, untenured—stops me from beginning this lecture where I want to begin—with myself—without the cloak of form (in this case a self-imposed skein of interrogatories)?

Alice Notley: Men who have written them [epics] since Homer have tended, or tried, to be near the center of the politics of their time, court or capitol. Thus, how could a woman write an epic?

3. How can I explain: what I care about is not just what someone says but how someone says it and who says it? How is this political?

Alice Notley: It's the only power I have.

4. Why do women need to tell their birth stories? Are birth stories women's war stories?

Alice Notley: It is essential that women like myself speak out.

5. Aside from telling stories—especially the stories which involve the fracture, dislocation, explosion of the self—is there any way to put one's self back together again, to become whole, to make sense of the moments in which we—you and I—are transformed into life-making or life-taking beings and become super- or subhuman—is there any anodyne or palliative for this fragmentation other than artmaking?

Alice Notley: This is the only power I have.

6. Perhaps poetry should not try to repair fragmentation but should move from the "I" to the self, which embraces and includes the "I" but which also includes the unconscious psyche and is an ideal greatness where everything is connected to everything else—is the "I" owned/invented by the patriarchy anyway?

Bernadette Mayer: The history of every historical thing including God but not including all men and women individually, is a violent mess like this ice. But for the spaces even hunchbacked history has allowed in between the famous and loud for something that's defined as what does please us. Which is perhaps the story of an intimate family, though you won't believe or will be unable to love it, driven to research love's limits in its present solitude as if each man or woman in the world was only one person with everything I've mentioned separate in him or she didn't represent history at all though he or she had stories to tell and was just sitting kind of crazily before an open window in midwinter.

7. Am I saying that the self is always male and female and neither but the "I" is almost always male? White? Dominant? Straight? That to speak or write as we have known it is to put on that mantle of authority, and what does this have to do with poetry or with government?

Alice Notley: I don't have a lyric voice anymore.

8. Does this appease or inflame the student who recently accused me of re-inforcing a gender binary that no longer exists or another student who tried to convince me we live in a post-racial world?

9. Am I a token female?

Alice Notley: No woman is like Helen, no matter what the male poets say . . . Only men are like them, in the sense that they invented them—they are pieces of the male mind.

10. Do I dare call attention to our whiteness? Straightness? Who would like to be the first to accuse me of identity politics? Which is greater: the danger of speaking for others or the danger of keeping silent? Why have we been allowed to speak? Chosen? Listened to?

Bernadette Mayer: What but the impulse to move and speak / Can change the world / Where should we move / Who is this person speaking / Who am I speaking to / To you whom I love, / Can I say that?

11. If I was writing poems before I had children, why do I say now that motherhood was the crisis that informed/inspired my real work and that now, though I am still primarily, fundamentally, eternally a mother first and foremost and forever, that the crisis of motherhood has ebbed and truly I find the need to speak diminished, blunted? What, retrospectively, does this prove about the need to speak?

Alicia Ostriker: But who can tolerate the power of a woman / close to a child, riding our tides / into the sand dunes of the public spaces.

12. Why do women need to tell their birth stories? Are we healing ourselves or the culture? Was/is anyone listening?

Tillie Olsen: Traces of their making, of course, in folk song, lullaby, tales, language itself, jokes, maxims, superstitions . . .

13. If Alice Notley is my patronus, why does she not appear as a female stag with golden antlers and carry me away from this panel?

14. Why is there no name for the birth poem when we have "elegy" for death? What if I refuse to tell you what to think? Or what I think? Why should I tell this in order or make an argument or prove my point with evidence? Who invented that form? Why did the culture tell me not to say? Not to tell it? And why must I, if I must, tell it slant?

Bernadette Mayer: From dreams I made sentences, then what I've seen today, / Then past the past of afternoons of stories like memory / To seeing a plain introduction of modes of love and reason, / Then to end I guess with love, a method to this winter season

15. Why, when I had already read *Stealing the Language* (Alicia Ostriker) and *Writing Like a Woman* (Ostriker) and *Of Woman Born* (Adrienne Rich) did it take cowriting a book about giving birth at home and subverting the "I" voice of single authorship for me to see that I'd been speaking, always, in a borrowed language and premade forms?

16. Why did I not see, until writing an overtly polemical book—see the women crying in the audiences and the scorn of young male graduate students at Prairie Lights and the pushback and anger and confusion and the gratitude—how thoroughly I had been dissuaded from writing about something, from writing politically, in a political manner which is to say of/for/about people and power, which is to say also female, a feministic diatribe meant to effect social change and name names?

Alice Notley: Perhaps this time she wouldn't call herself something like Helen; perhaps instead there might be recovered some sense of what mind was like before Homer, before the world went haywire & women were denied participation in the design & making of it.

17. Did I think that reimagining the story of Persephone from a female point of view had political value? Did I think telling the story of my second son's birth in all the mess and glory and dislocation in a way I had never seen birth described before in a poem had political relevance? Did I think telling

the "true" story of (my) wifehood and motherhood was political? Did I think spending years collecting essays by young women poets about their female mentors in order to describe a permission-giving influence rather than a "kill the father" model would change anything/anyone? Did I think asking ninety-nine poets to write a poem for one of Obama's first one hundred days of presidency would make me a responsible poet-citizen? Would make me part of the political process?

18. How did I feel when I realized the birth I had described was mine and also the birth given to me by a patriarchal system of medicine that despises women's bodies? How did I feel when the mentorship book was dismissed as too anecdotal and unscholarly and could not find a place in the academic male-storm? How did I feel when I realized that the Obama poem project, while "community-building," and about government, mostly failed to be political in its making or reception?

19. Why should you care how I feel, or how anyone feels? Does caring about someone's feelings have anything to do with politics or poetry? What is the voice of a woman? A white woman, a straight, Jewish-American woman—and why does it matter who is speaking and how can it not matter?

20. If everyone were busy caring for someone—a child, a parent, a friend, a person in need, or even one's self, in a deep way—would we then have no time or energy left for war? What would government be without the possibility of war—can you even imagine? Do you have the language to imagine? Do you have the need, the right, the privilege, the method, the desire to speak?

■ ■ ■

"a homespun of questions pulled over a loom of gender and race with the voices of ancestral (mostly living) women speaking in the lacunae" was written for a panel called "The Need to Speak: Writing the Political Poem" for the Association of Writing Programs conference. I was invited by Joe Wilkins, a poet I did not know, and gladly agreed to be listed on the panel proposal because the topic of political poetry as well as the title "The Need to Speak" were of great interest to me. I found it curious and a bit misguided that the hopeful moderator had chosen three men —C. K. Williams, Robert Wrigley and Matthew Zapruder—and one woman (myself) to list on his proposal. I suspected that either Matthew Zapruder or Robert Wrigley had suggested me to Joe, and I wondered whether I was the token female. One of the other panelists joked about how our last names all started with letters at the far end of the alphabet. The joke made me think about how none of us were remarking to one another what else we had in common—we were all white and also (as far as I knew) all straight. The panel was accepted and as the conference grew nearer I became increasingly preoccupied with the straight-white-almost-entirely-maleness of our panel. I was also, honestly, nervous about going up on stage with poets who had achieved a kind of authority in the field that I have not. I admire these poets' work, am friendly with Matthew and Robert (I'd never met C. K. Williams) and still, as the time grew near, I felt increasingly unlike them—more self-conscious about my inclusion in this group and more suspicious of my own anxiety.

What, I wondered, would "the men" talk about? I wondered if they would talk about war or about other male poets. I felt a self-imposed responsibility to somehow balance what I imagined they might say, to somehow bring a different (feminine?) perspective to the discussion. The stakes seemed high to me, and I became more and more unable to formulate a thesis or point of view—I could not find my voice of authority. I wanted to get up and say something smart and convincing even though I suspected that my age, gender, stature, reputation, non-tenure-track status would make it difficult for me to compete with these men. But, why, I began to wonder, was impressing the audience the goal? Why was I searching for authority or authoritativeness? In my teaching, writing, mothering, and living I was not grasping for authority. I was not hoping to bend another's will to mine, to overpower anyone (physically or mentally). I was not in the business of trying to impose my worldview. I was trying, more and more, to listen, to ask, to be aware of the relationships between myself and others, myself and the environment. So, why then was I suddenly trying to do the equivalent of putting on a business suit for a job interview? To be clear, Joe, Matthew, C. K., and Robert weren't asking me to do anything or be anything or act in any particular way. All of these expectations were self-imposed.

Even when writing prose I often begin with a notion of shape rather than an idea, and after weeks and weeks the only thing I knew was that I would only allow myself to ask questions because somehow this felt like a way of subverting the norms of panel presentations and also (hopefully) might at least draw awareness to the problematic nature of four men and one woman—all white and straight—telling a room full of people what to think about politics and poetry or the political poem or the need to speak. I was also aware of not wanting to directly address or offend the other panelists who had done nothing wrong, who could not be blamed for being male or white or straight or agreeing to be on the panel.

I was also aware that I was spending a lot of time worrying about the other panelists' feelings, about the moderator's feelings, about the feelings of my imagined audience, and I wondered if the other panelists were doing the same.

But a formal notion and a set of worries is not a panel presentation. I had the idea of questions and some of the questions, but it felt like nothing. I arrived in Chicago the day before my panel and rushed from the airport to the conference; I made it just in time to see Alice Notley give a reading and answer questions. I have long adored Notley's work and she was, on that day, magnificent. She was brazen, unapologetic, and refused to answer the questions posed to her by her interviewer. Her fierceness was a shot of courage for me and gave me the idea to include the words of my poetic foremothers (including Notley) without analyzing them. I wanted to let them speak, to call them forth to gather around me, to keep me safe, or to help me not care about being safe.

I was the last to speak. I do not wish to malign the other panelists who, as I've said, are my friends and who I genuinely admire. They each said interesting things and spoke about politics and poetry in smart, resonant ways. They also each made certain choices individually that highlighted some of the problems of our panel. Three of them spoke only of other male poets. One of them quite authoritatively made the claim that the greatest political poem ever was written by Robert Bly. They spoke primarily about war. They made grand, authoritative statements. I was interested in and impressed by their statements and close-readings of the poets they chose to highlight. I also noticed that I felt smaller and more female and less scholarly as they spoke. When it was my turn, I got up and read my piece without introduction. I felt certain that if I went "off script" it would end up being an apology, and I didn't want to apologize.

When I finished reading the audience began to clap, and as I looked up several rows were standing. I saw a few friends and poets I knew scattered about, but who were these strangers standing and clapping? Were they clapping for all of us or only for me? It dawned on me that I was receiving a standing ovation—the first of my life and perhaps the last—and I was very aware that my immediate emotional response was to cringe, to shrink, to apologize. It seemed to go on a long time and I was bizarrely aware of my own thoughts. I had shuffled to my seat and was keeping my eyes down. "Be Anne Waldman!!" a voice said in my head. "Look up and see it, take it in!" the strong voice said. "I can't," said a smaller voice. "Please stop clapping!" said the smaller voice. "Oh dear," said the small voice. I tried to look up, to "be Anne Waldman," but I could not. That small voice was too persistent. That small voice told me that the audience's response was due to some witchy manipulation on my part— "cheap shot!" said the small voice. "You used your femaleness (and Jewishness?) as a kind of sympathy card and have offended perfectly lovely poets who will now hate you," said the small voice. "Shut up!" said my mental version of Anne Waldman to the small voice, "shut up, small, shrinking, female fear-voice! You didn't tell them what to say or do and you're not in control of the audience's response! Take some pleasure and responsibility for your own power and let the rest go." The audience stopped clapping and sat down long before these voices stopped arguing. I've thought about that panel—writing my piece, speaking it, my response to the audience's response—for months and am still not sure what to make of it or make out of it.

2012

CONFESSIONALOGRAPHY

A GNAT (GROSSLY NONACADEMIC TALK) ON "I" IN POETRY

AN A/HISTORICAL PREVIEW

Poets have always used personal experience as subject matter for poems, but the emphasis on self, the effect of using "I" and the reader's expectation of the authenticity of personal information has shifted and changed over time. Shakespeare used the pronoun "I" and sometimes it was him and sometimes it probably wasn't. The Romantics wrote "personal poems," and their readers caught on to the fact that even when poets were writing about nature they were really writing about themselves. These Romantic selves wandered around the heath and through abbeys at times lonely like clouds, at other times punch drunk on the splendor of everything. Walt Whitman also wandered around proclaiming and expounding, while employing an "I" as big as the cosmos, as irrepressible as an avalanche. Then came T. S. Eliot, who wanted poetry to escape from personality and emotion. He probably didn't put much stock in the fact that one really important goal of a poem, according to Frank O'Hara, is to convince someone to have sex with you. After a while, American poets rebelled against Eliot. W. D. Snodgrass, Robert Lowell, Anne Sexton, Sylvia Plath, John Berryman, and Allen Ginsberg started to use personal information in a way that woke everyone up. The critic M. L. Rosenthal described this poetry as "confessional," and people spent a lot of time arguing about who was or wasn't confessional, and what really made a poem "confessional."

Being "confessional" had something to do with breaking taboos, suffering, and claiming that the "self" of the poem was not "a speaker" but was actually the poet. It was a catchy name—"confessional poetry"—and it also meant that high school students didn't have to spend as much time looking for symbols in poems and could, with no training at all, write really bad poems that helped them "express" themselves. Of course, there were a few problems. For one, was this poetry really radically new? A century earlier, Emily Dickinson had written searingly personal poems—poems in which the disclosure of self is so raw and painful you can almost feel her skin come off—and Allen Ginsberg's "I" sounds a whole lot like Walt Whitman's "I." Yet, people felt that these "confessional" poems were unlike anything ever written before, though no one could say exactly how they were different, and the poets themselves made this more difficult because no one wanted to be counted in or left out.

The second problem was that everyone remembers Mother saying "no one likes a whiner!" which was annoying until you're in the presence of a true whiner and realize that Mother was right. Bad confessional poetry was even worse than bad Romantic poetry, and just as poets used to be scared of sounding academic and ivory tower, now they were scared of sounding too much like New-Age-mantra posters. Also, if people are only focused on the content of the poems, what happens to form and craft and language? What about using language not simply as a vehicle for subject matter, but as a supernal medium in and of itself?

Afterwards and meanwhile, some people wrote Language poetry and tried to empty the signs of meaning and talk about "speech acts." With their collages and their games and their abstractions, they were struggling with language so intimately that this was a kind of suffering as well, a deep suffering, but most readers couldn't see this, couldn't feel this because it sounded so damn intellectualized and abstract.

Where were the subjects, not just the nouns? Readers wanted to know, "Goddammit, where had all the human beings gone and what happened to love and sex and emotion and drugs?" And young poets (dare this author say especially young women poets) started wondering, "Wait a second, why can't I say 'I'? Shakespeare did!" And then came ellipticism, post-Language, lyric, new narrativity, post-postmodern (look these up to little avail and at your own peril) until poets, or shall I simply say "I," began to struggle with how to write a poetry that is truthful and about the self and uses "I," a poetry that admits that things happen and people happen and emotions are real and important, if not essential components of Art, and that the body (MY BODY) is involved, inextricable from language. At the same time, "I" has DOUBT and IDEAS and SKEPTICISM and ATHEISM, and so it is no longer so easy to write about the body and love and sex and belief without acknowledging that "I" is complicit, that people have killed each other over such matters, and that the struggle to be both personal and political and honest and convincing is no small or minor matter.

And then we have the history of confessional poetry as a specific movement or group of poets, the effects of language as propaganda and beauty, as a threshold to ethnic cleansing, and maybe I don't really want to kill myself and maybe even though I admit that I love Sharon Olds for her courage and candor and bloody show, I still don't want to be put in her party, her group, her post-confessional or neo-confessional prototype because I also believe in privacy, because surgery is not an act of intimacy. It's not easy to make useful objects that are also finely woven, especially when clothes are so cheap nowadays and the looms are intimidating.

SHORT QUIZ TO DETERMINE WHETHER OR NOT YOU ARE A CONFESSIONAL POET

1. Are you Robert Lowell?
2. Do you feel, like Whitman, that you are a part of the world?
3. Do you feel that your circumstances, sufferings or joys make you distinct, separate, unusual?
4. Do you dislike the poetry of Robert Lowell?
5. Are you an American?
6. Has anyone ever accused you of being self-absorbed?
7. Do you feel it is ethical to reveal personal material about your spouse, family, friends or enemies?
8. Do you feel it is unethical to pretend to be someone other—either worse or better—than you actually are; in other words, is it unethical to present a fictional self with the sheen of accuracy?
9. Do you believe that poetry should transform the mundane, the real, the banal into something spiritual, transcendent, ephemeral or do you feel that poetry should report reality which is already excruciatingly transcendent and strange and incongruous?
10. Have you ever committed suicide?

Scoring: Give yourself one point for every "yes." Give yourself an extra 1,000 if you answered "yes" to question #1.

If you scored over 1,000 then you ARE a CONFESSIONAL POET.

If you scored between 1–1000 you might or might not be a CONFESSIONAL POET and should write to M. L. Rosenthal for guidance.

SOME THOUGHTS ABOUT THE CURRENT CLIMATE/TENETS OF, LET'S CALL IT, CONFESSIONALISTIC POETRY

1. Autobiographical poetry doesn't exist. If it did exist it would be the pure reportage of a poet's biographical information set down as verse. The closest thing we have to autobiographical poetry is the blog-in-verse, but even blogs are subject to the Heisenberg uncertainty principle.

2. Let us call the use of stories and "facts" from a poet's life "autobiographicality." Autobiographicality demands, expects, and preimagines an audience; it is social even when it describes the antisocial. When the autobiographicalistic poet finds his own information so utterly fascinating that he falls in love with the story of his own life, the result is an ode or elegy to the self. The poem looks like the infinitely repeating reflection in the corner of a mirrored dressing room.

3. Autobiographicality is often exculpatory and can be therapeutic; narrative is an anodyne for existential despair. Telling your life story helps you unburden, repent, and see the self as woven into narrative. Autobiographicality is therefore narcissistic and self-preservative. This is not necessarily bad. It is okay, for example, for poets to stay alive. It is important, however, to remember that staying alive through writing is not the same as "expressing" yourself. If we were rigorous in reserving the

self-reflexive use of the verb "to express" to describe a lactating woman in the process of manually "expressing" milk from her breasts, we would realize that most poets, no matter how autobiographicalistic, are not expressing themselves. Breast milk expressed into the sink or onto a washcloth runs down the drain or is invisibly absorbed, whereas telling and certainly writing are their own containers. Poetry has staying power (as Paul Valéry said: "Poetry is language that does not die for having lived"); expression disappears into memory.

4. Autobiographicality, even when inspired by narcissism, is often enjoyed by the reader/listener. First of all, people like hearing about other people's lives. Tabloids, *E! True Hollywood Story*, biographies, and pornography all pander to our natural voyeurism. But, unlike these other forms of commercial art, autobiographicality in poetry is a show of respect for the reader, a kind of humility not just humanity-on-display. Think of it as the difference between how a storyteller makes eye contact with the audience and how an actor pretends the audience isn't there. The autobiographicalistic poet is aware of the audience and doesn't pretend otherwise.

5. Autobiographicality often reminds the audience of poetry's social mission. The stories of self gain oppressive power when kept taboo. Telling "the truth" about life is liberation from this oppression. The stories of childbirth, of boredom, of sexuality, etc., need to be told and can be told powerfully in poems.

6. Let us now define another poetry, I'll call it "confessionalistic," a silly sounding term I use only in order to distinguish this poetry from the

school of poetry previously called confessional. Confessionalistic poetry may include confessional poetry but is not limited to any particular era or group of poets.

7. Confessionalistic poetry is not a "school" or type, but is rather a degree or tonality. Confessionalistic poems include moments of autobiographicality but also have qualities and aspirations that not all autobiographicalistic poems have. Autobiographicality is a subset of confessionalistic poetry. Not all autobiographicalistic poems are confessionalistic. In fact, autobiographicality can often be used to mask the lack of self-reflection that confessionalistic poetry demands.

8. What then does confessionalistic poetry have that autobiographicality lacks? Confessionalistic poetry reaches for the universal. It attempts to transcend the personal, the particular, not because it is embarrassed by the particulars, and the personal, but because, ultimately, confessionalistic poetry uses the bits and elements of story in the service of larger subjects, subjects that are not limited to particularities of the poet's life. This is not to say that the self becomes symbolic as it did in Romantic poetry, but, rather, that the self is always overcome, overwhelmed, disturbed.

9. There needs to be risk. Confessionalistic poetry is more risky than autobiographicality. Autobiographicality, no matter how disturbing the content, is always the story of a life, of what happened, of circumstance and event. Confessionalistic poetry is the splitting open of self, a minor chord before and without resolution. A shopping list read aloud, even with gusto, with style, is not confessionalistic, even if you intend to buy

parmesan, pull-ups, and heroin. The risk in a poem that relies heavily on autobiographicality is usually a risk of content. Privacy, reputation, and decency, may all be risked by the autobiographicalistic poet. But the confessionalistic poet risks more; she is willing to undermine the boundaries of self. Often, she is writing at the frayed edge of the genre in the busy interstitial space between neurons.

10. As we are pulled downstream by these swirling "isms" and "alistics," I offer, as a piece of floating driftwood, Jorie Graham's poem "Imperialism." Graham's poem is made of personal detail, a mosaic of scenes and stories presented in the mode of autobiographical truth. A husband and wife, illuminated by a kerosene lamp, exchange cruelties. But the poem is not about the husband and wife. It is not even about how narrative comes to colonize these real people, the Brentwood chair, the linoleum, the poet, the stories the poet wants to tell or how ideas come to colonize the self. Narrative is nothing without them, these details and people, these subjects who sit and try to nail point of view into the world, but the poem reaches for a force that is more powerful than narrative. The poem tells a story the poet cannot tell. A story about the river Ganges. It is a story (river) full of bodies, knives, newborn calves, utensils, genitals, even the ashes of the recently cremated. The story is about the catastrophe of knowing the world and about the impossibility of trying to get clean in thick muddy water. The poet only manages to tell the part of the story about a man washing a white umbrella in that brown river. What the poem is really about you will have to decide for yourself. I will say only that it is clear that the umbrella, the marriage, the poet, the linoleum, the river, the Mother, the "irrelevant" body of the Mother, are not symbolic but real, autobiographical. It is also and equally clear

that this poem, while it uses bits of personal detail and elements of story is not about the poet's life. The poem is not about anything she is using to make the poem.

11. Now I will use a ridiculous analogy that I will later disavow and vociferously swear was inserted here by the editors of this publication: Romantic poetry is the lightness of a soufflé about to fall. Autobiographical poetry is a raw egg with or without salmonella. Autobiographicality is a hard-boiled egg with or without a beginning art student in the background practicing chiaroscuro. Confessional poetry is a hard-boiled egg with a serrated knife lodged in its center and a tiny tear drop of blood on the knife's handle. Confessionalistic poetry is half a deviled egg, with no sign of the other half except a thin snow drift of paprika on the white plate.

12. Many poems I would consider confessionalistic sound and function nothing at all like Jorie Graham's work. Some confessionalistic poems (Frank O'Hara's work comes to mind) appear to reveal the self accidentally. The content may not explicitly deal with matters of self and self-disclosure, but the effect of writing the poem is profoundly revealing. The autobiographicalistic poet may call himself a dirty name, but will ultimately reveal less than what the handwriting (or signature meters) of a confessionalistic poet may expose.

13. Whereas autobiographicality is most often declamatory, confessionalistic poetry has a wide range of volumes. It can sound like the self overheard or can be almost silent: the sound of the walk of a man who has spent his life in the cavalry.

14. "I" is capitalized because it is not only a name, but because it is also an idea and now, perhaps, a movement like Romanticism. "I" is the name I call myself, and "I" is also the idea of self. As such, confessionalistic poets attempt to engage the public interest, the public truth through material that always involves private experience.

15. The backlash against self-indulgence led to a disavowal of the personal, the needlessly profane, the sensational. But it is important to remember that we learn—nipple in mouth—through sensation and all our ideas are formed from shapes and colors and textures and urgent feelings. Without the personal, without visceral knowledge, without empathy, we are (and I mean this literally) anti-social fundamentalist murderers.

16. There is no need to fear the personal or the confessional. For one thing, it is unavoidable. For another thing, it is all you have. Penultimately, it can save you. Lastly, you can never really, fully, and honestly tell the truth about your own life because a) you don't know the truth b) there is no one truth and c) you are always telling, and telling the truth is very different from the truth. Think of it this way: If you take your clothes off you are naked but are not a Nude, and certainly not a nude painting. The poem, no matter how bare, is a Nude, and never really naked. That said, you need to take your clothes off to know what your skin really feels like.

17. Take your clothes off.

2014

RACHEL ZUCKER ON HER
BOOK *SOUNDMACHINE*

When I tell people I'm a poet, they almost always respond, "What kind of poetry do you write?" Considering how many times I've been asked this question, it's still surprisingly difficult to answer. Here are a few of the responses I've offered over the past twenty-five years:

"I write about my kids and family and body and life . . . it doesn't rhyme."

"Good poetry?"

"Sorta like Sylvia Plath but without the whole head in-the-oven part . . . so far anyway."

"I write about things women aren't supposed to talk about: sex, marriage, childbirth, childrearing, female desire, female rage, depression, anxiety . . . it makes me super popular."

"I write long poems that tell stories, usually stories about me."

"Unmarketable memoir. My books would all be bestsellers if not for the line breaks."

"I write observational comedy that isn't funny."

The last response is plagiarized from a comment my husband, Josh Goren, made about my work. It wasn't an insult—and, in case you were wondering, a lot of my work is funny or at least tragicomic. My husband, whose name, used as a verb, means "to joke," is a huge fan of comedy, and he was observing that my writing is closer to stand-up comedy than lyric poetry.

Lately, I've considered asking the next person who asks me what kind of poetry I write if they've seen the TV series *The Marvelous Mrs. Maisel*. Like Midge Maisel, I'm a Jewish mother fighting against the reviled caricature of "The Jewish Mother." Like Midge, I attended a fancy college and live on the Upper West Side. Like Midge, I'm a lot: talkative, ambitious, sensitive, full of outrage and love, and I make an extremely excellent brisket (I challenge any reader to a brisket contest). Did I mention I'm battling the stereotype of the Jewish Mother?

Like Midge, I speak very openly (obsessively?) about my marriage and children. Midge's husband often feels eclipsed by her (as does mine), but is ultimately more in love with her and her ability than he is aggrieved that he's not the brightest star in the family (as, thankfully, is mine). Midge's father is hurt and angry with her for exposing him in one of her routines. My mother's last words to me (relayed to me by her therapist) on the way to the hospital for emergency heart surgery from which she did not wake up were: "Tell Rachel not to publish the book." My mother was talking about my book *MOTHERs*, which was, in part, about her, and which I did publish despite her dying wish. The fact that I just told you that story gives you some sense of what kind of poet I am. It's a true story. I probably shouldn't have just told it. And it's not really funny. In fact, it's really not funny.

Most of the pieces in my latest book, *SoundMachine*, don't have line breaks and read as prose. I write about trying to explain death to my son as he's falling asleep, about grief and loss, about my very long marriage, about my sons' mental health struggles, about the boredom, restlessness, and suffocation of motherhood, about the excruciating, powerless responsibility of motherhood, and the struggle to make a home for my family and maintain a part of my soul, self, body, and psyche that is not a wife and mother. I write about loving my children so much that I almost can't but must endure the violence, hatred, toxicity, and precarity of our daily lives. I write about our political climate, the looming threat of environmental catastrophe, about insidiousness of white supremacy, toxic masculinity, and the heteropatriarchy, none of which I find funny even if humor is essential to our survival of these forces.

No one really knows what makes something funny, and what's funny to one person isn't necessarily funny to another. But provocation, making public what should remain private, voicing or describing something forbidden, and breaking taboos are often essential elements of humor. These are also elements of confessional poetry, which isn't often funny. But, if I'm saying I do those things but no one laughs, and I'm saying I'm not that into Sylvia Plath, why do I do it?

I was raised to believe that *lashon hara* (gossip) is a serious injury and that honoring your parents is so important it supersedes "thou shalt not kill" in the ten commandments, but I was not raised with the sacrament of confession, the notion of original sin, or the Christian view that my thoughts were sins for which I should repent. Instead, Talmudic argument, midrash, and storytelling were at the heart of my upbringing, and openly expressing my feelings and ideas, even if these thoughts and emotions were difficult or unsavory, was encouraged.

Many of my favorite writers (and my parents' favorite writers) use words to challenge repressive social norms. There is a lot of freedom for a provocateur in having been raised this way and in being praised for emulating artists who struggle with the ethics of speaking up, speaking out, speaking against, speaking about—whose art renders them exposed and naked and exposes the oppressive forces around us. Lenny Bruce, Spalding Gray, Sharon Olds, Adrienne Rich, Alicia Ostriker, Allen Ginsberg, Wayne Koestenbaum, Tig Notaro, Ali Wong, Alice Notley, Toi Derricotte, Bernadette Mayer, Art Spiegelman, Audre Lorde, Joy Harjo, David Berman, Anne Sexton, Sacha Baron Cohen, Alison Bechdel (to name just a few of my influences) are truth-tellers, risk-takers, and poets in the sense that they are re-makers of forms.

I could tell people that I'm "a straight lady (pun intended) Allen Ginsberg." I love Ginsberg's poetry, but, like Midge, I'm no beatnik (yet?). Too many kids, more than two decades of monotony, oops, I meant monogamy, a day job, no acid trips. I enjoy a good rant, but, unlike Ginsberg, I'm not very prophetic in my poetics.

The thing is, Mrs. Maisel may be marvelous, but she didn't exist. I do. My fashion sense is deplorable, my children are constantly interrupting me, and no one has ever described me as "marvelous." The fictional character of Midge uses foul language and talks about things women were/are not supposed to talk about, but she's not telling it like it is, and the show is a whitewashing of racism, misogyny, class differences, and the sociopolitical reality of the 1950s. (For two great responses to the show read Emily Nussbaum in the *New Yorker* and Rokhl Kafrissen in *Alma*.)

It's not a very snappy answer, but I write the kind of poetry that proves I exist, that I—a daughter, wife, and mother living a life of great privilege and difficulty at a moment in history when my body is both cherished and reviled, empowered and corseted by my gender, guided by (and away from) Jewish belief and sensibility—tried to love and care for others and tried to speak the truth, even when it wasn't funny.

2020

SELECTED BIBLIOGRAPHY

AND WORKS CITED

Ammons, A. R. *Tape for the Turn of the Year*. New York: W. W. Norton, 1965.

Atwood, Margaret. *Power Politics*. Toronto: House of Anansi Press, 1971.

Badia, Janet. "The 'Priestess' and Her 'Cult': Plath's Confessional Poetics and the Mythology of Women Readers." In *The Unraveling Archive: Essays on Sylvia Plath*. Edited by Anita Helle, 159–81. Ann Arbor, MI: University of Michigan Press, 2007.

Bell, Marvin. *Nightworks: Poems, 1962–2000*. Port Townsend, WA: Copper Canyon Press, 2000.

Bell, Pearl. "Poets of Our Times." *The New Leader*, vol. 58 (May 1975).

Berryman, John. *The Dream Songs*. New York: Farrar, Straus & Giroux, 1969.

Burt, Stephanie. "Review: *Smokes* by Susan Wheeler." *Boston Review* (June 1, 1998).

Clifton, Lucille. *The Book of Light*. Port Townsend, WA: Copper Canyon Press, 1992.

Culler, Jonathan. "Lyric, History, and Genre." *New Literary History* 40, no. 4 (Autumn 2009): 879–99.

Davey, Moyra, ed. *Mother Reader: Essential Writings on Motherhood*. New York: Seven Stories Press, 2001.

Derricotte, Toi. *Tender*. Pittsburgh, PA: University of Pittsburgh Press, 1997.

———. *Natural Birth*. Ann Arbor, MI: Firebrand Books, 2000.

Diaz, Natalie. *When My Brother Was an Aztec*. Port Townsend, WA: Copper Canyon Press, 2012.

Dickinson, Emily. *The Poems of Emily Dickinson: Reading Edition*. Edited by R. W.

Franklin. Cambridge, MA: The Belknap Press of Harvard University Press, 2005.

Ewing, Eve L. "Eve Ewing vs. the Apocalypse." Interview with Franny Choi and Danez Smith, *VS* podcast (June 15, 2017).

Foucault, Michel. "Discourse and Truth." Lecture, University of California, Berkeley, 1983.

Fries, Kenny. "Beauty and Variations." In *Beauty is a Verb: The New Poetry of Disability*. Edited by Jennifer Bartlett, Sheila Black, and Michael Northen, 107–09. El Paso, TX: Cinco Puntos Press, 2011.

Gilbert, Sandra M. "'My Name Is Darkness': The Poetry of Self-Definition." *Contemporary Literature* 18, no. 4 (1977): 443–57.

Ginsberg, Allen. *Collected Poems, 1947–1980*. New York: HarperCollins, 1984.

Heaney, Seamus. *North*. London: Faber & Faber, 1975.

Hillman, Brenda. "Split, Spark, and Space." In *The Grand Permission: New Writings on Poetics and Motherhood*. Edited by Patricia Dienstfrey and Brenda Hillman, 245–54. Middletown, CT: Wesleyan University Press, 2003.

Jordan, June. *Directed by Desire: The Collected Poems of June Jordan*. Edited by Jan Heller Levi and Sara Miles. Port Townsend, WA: Copper Canyon Press, 2005.

Keats, John. *The Complete Poems of John Keats*. New York: Modern Library, 1994.

Kuusisto, Stephen. "Lyric Anger and the Victrola in the Attic." Interview with Ralph Savarese. *Journal of Literary & Cultural Disability Studies* 3.2 (2009).

Lewis, Robin Coste. *Voyage of the Sable Venus and Other Poems* (reprint edition). New York: Knopf, 2017.

Lorde, Audre. *The Black Unicorn*. New York: W. W. Norton, 1978.

———. *The Collected Poems of Audre Lorde*. New York: W. W. Norton, 1997.

———. *Sister Outsider: Essays and Speeches*. New York: Crossing Press, 1984.

Lowell, Robert. *The Dolphin*. New York: Farrar, Straus & Giroux, 1973.

———. *The Letters of Robert Lowell*. Edited by Saskia Hamilton. New York: Farrar, Straus & Giroux, 2005.

———. *Life Studies*. New York: Farrar, Straus & Cudahy, 1959.

————. *Selected Poems*. New York: Farrar, Straus & Giroux, 1977.

Mayer, Bernadette. *Midwinter Day*. New York: New Directions, 1999.

Merwin, W. S. *The Second Four Books of Poems*. Port Townsend, WA: Copper Canyon Press, 1992.

Moore, Honor, ed. *Poems from the Women's Movement*. New York: Library of America, 2009.

Moore, Marianne. *The Complete Poems of Marianne Moore*. New York: Macmillan, 1967.

Murillo, John. "Family Business: Elegy and the Ethics of Confession." Lecture, Adelphi University, 2014.

Nelson, Deborah. *Pursuing Privacy in Cold War America*. New York: Columbia University Press, 2002.

Nelson, Maggie. *The Red Parts*. Minneapolis: Graywolf Press, 2016.

Notley, Alice. Association of Writers and Writing Programs reading and conversation (March 1, 2012).

————. *Grave of Light: New and Selected Poems, 1970–2005*. Middletown, CT: Wesleyan University Press, 2006.

————. *Incidentals in the Day World*. New York: Angel Hair Books, 1973.

————. "The Poetics of Disobedience." Lecture, The Poetry Foundation, May 15, 2010.

————. "*PW* Talks with Alice Notley." Interview with Brian Kim Stefans. *Publishers Weekly* (August 27, 2001).

Olds, Sharon. *The Gold Cell*. New York: Alfred A. Knopf, 1987.

————. *Odes*. New York: Alfred A. Knopf, 2016.

————. *Satan Says*. Pittsburgh, PA: University of Pittsburgh Press, 1980.

————. *Stag's Leap: Poems*. New York: Alfred A. Knopf, 2012.

Olsen, Tillie. *Silences*. New York: The Feminist Press at CUNY, 2003.

Ostriker, Alicia. *The Mother/Child Papers*. Boston: Beacon Press, 1986.

————. *Stealing the Language: The Emergence of Women's Poetry in America*. Boston: Beacon Press, 1987.

———. *Writing Like a Woman.* Ann Arbor, MI: University of Michigan Press, 1983.

Plath, Sylvia. *Ariel.* New York: Harper & Row, 1966.

———. *The Collected Poems.* New York: Harper & Row, 1981.

Rankine, Claudia. *Citizen: An American Lyric.* Minneapolis: Graywolf Press, 2014.

———. *Don't Let Me Be Lonely: An American Lyric.* Saint Paul, MN: Graywolf Press, 2004.

Rich, Adrienne. *Of Woman Born: Motherhood as Experience and Institution.* New York: W. W. Norton, 1976.

Rosenthal, M. L. *Our Life in Poetry: Selected Essays and Reviews.* New York: Persea Books, 1991.

Roth, Philip. *American Pastoral.* Boston: Houghton Mifflin, 1997.

Rukeyser, Muriel. *The Collected Poems of Muriel Rukeyser.* Edited by Janet E. Kaufman and Anne F. Herzog, with Jan Heller Levi. Pittsburgh, PA: University of Pittsburgh Press, 2005.

Schott, Webster. "The Cult of Plath." *Washington Post* "Book World" (October 1, 1972).

Sexton, Anne. *The Complete Poems.* Boston: Houghton Mifflin, 1981.

Shivani, Anis. "The 15 Most Overrated Contemporary American Writers." *The Huffington Post,* 2010.

Smiley, Jane. "Can Mothers Think?" In *The True Subject: Writers on Life and Craft.* Edited by Kurt Brown. Saint Paul, MN: Graywolf Press, 1993.

Umansky, Lauri. *Motherhood Reconceived: Feminism and the Legacies of the Sixties.* New York: New York University Press, 1996.

Vap, Sarah. *End of the Sentimental Journey.* Las Cruces, NM: Noemi Press, 2013.

Vendler, Helen. "Malevolent Flippancy." In *Anne Sexton: Telling the Tale.* Edited by Steven E. Colburn. Ann Arbor, MI: University of Michigan Press, 1988.

———. *The Music of What Happens: Poems, Poets, Critics.* Cambridge, MA: Harvard University Press, 1988.

Whitman, Walt. *Leaves of Grass*. New York: Bantam Books, 2004.

Wood, Susan. "Words for Dr. Y: Uncollected Poems by Anne Sexton," *Washington Post* "Book World" (October 15, 1978).

Wright, C. D. *Cooling Time: An American Poetry Vigil*. Port Townsend, WA: Copper Canyon Press, 2005.

———. "In a Ring of Cows Is the Signal Given: Ruminations on Mothering and Writing." In *The Grand Permission: New Writings on Poetics and Motherhood*, edited by Patricia Dienstfrey and Brenda Hillman. Middletown, CT: Wesleyan University Press, 2003.

Zeisler, Andi. *We Were Feminists Once: From Riot Grrrl to CoverGirl®, the Buying and Selling of a Political Movement*. New York: PublicAffairs, 2016.

ACKNOWLEDGMENTS

The Bagley Wright Lecture Series on Poetry supports contemporary poets as they explore in depth their own thinking on poetry and poetics and give a series of lectures resulting from these investigations.

This work evolved from lectures given at the following institutions and organizations: "The Poetics of Wrongness, an Unapologia," Library of Congress, Washington, DC, December 4, 2015; "What We Talk about When We Talk about the Confessional and What We SHOULD Be Talking About," University of Arizona Poetry Center, Tucson, AZ, January 28, 2016; "What We Talk about When We Talk about the Confessional and What We SHOULD Be Talking About," Princeton University, Princeton, NJ, February 3, 2016; "A Very Large Charge: The Ethics of 'Say Everything' Poetry," New York University, New York, NY, February 5, 2016; "What We Talk about When We Talk about the Confessional and What We SHOULD Be Talking About," University of Pittsburgh, Pittsburgh, PA, February 11, 2016; "A Very Large Charge: The Ethics of 'Say Everything' Poetry," University of Texas at Austin, Austin, TX, February 17, 2016; "Poetry and Photography," Yale University, New Haven, CT, March 9, 2016; "What We Talk about When We Talk about the Confessional and What We SHOULD Be Talking About," The Poetry Foundation, Chicago, IL, April 28, 2016; "What We Talk about When We Talk about the Confessional and What We SHOULD Be Talking About," The Laundromat at the Ace Hotel, Portland, OR, November 11, 2016; "The Poetics of Wrongness, an Unapologia," Seattle Arts & Lectures, Seattle, WA, November 14, 2016; "Why She Could Not Write a Lecture on the Poetics of Motherhood," University of California, Berkeley, Berkeley, CA, November 15, 2016.

Thank you to Rob Casper and Anya Creightney at the Library of Congress; Tyler Meier and Hannah Ensor at the University of Arizona Poetry Center; Cate L. Mahoney at Princeton University; Joanna Yas and Soren P. Stockman at New York University; Yona Harvey and Sten Carlson at University of Pittsburgh; Lisa Olstein at University of Texas at Austin; Karin Roffman and Laura Wexler at Yale University; Stephen Young, Elizabeth Burke-Dain, and Polly Faust at The Poetry Foundation; Susan Moore at Portland Literary Arts; Rebecca Hoogs and Alison Stagner at Seattle Arts & Lectures; and C. S. Giscombe, Robert Hass, and Jane Gregory at University of California at Berkeley; as well as all of their respective teams, for welcoming the Bagley Wright Lecture Series into their programming and for collaborating on these events. The Series would be impossible without such partnerships.

NOTE FROM THE AUTHOR

More Dedications

"The Poetics of Wrongness, an Unapologia" is for Erin Murray Marra, who gave me the space to write this lecture and with whom I've been discussing wrongness for more than two decades.

"What We Talk about When We Talk about the Confessional and What We SHOULD Be Talking About" is for Arielle Greenberg, heart-sister, cheerleader, collaborator, life coach.

"A Very Large Charge: The Ethics of 'Say Everything' Poetry" is for Sharon Olds, beacon, dancer, friend.

"Why She Could Not Write a Lecture on the Poetics of Motherhood" is for my sons—Moses Zucker Goren, Abram Benjamin Zucker Goren, and Judah Darwin Zucker Goren. I love you first, foremost, and forever.

More Thank-Yous

Bagley Wright Lecture Series—Charlie Wright and Matthew Zapruder—for offering me the daunting privilege to think deeply about poetry in front of and with a live audience. And to Ellen Welcker for her support, encouragement, and organizational acumen.

Each and every audience member who attended my lectures. Your questions, comments, challenges, support, and encouragement made these lectures feel like conversations, which is always what I want and always what I strive for. I was and am deeply honored by your attention.

Each and every *Commonplace* guest (there are over 105 of you by now!) for your time, attention, vulnerability, and companionship.

The Poetry Center at the University of Arizona for resources, support, encouragement, and time, especially Hannah Ensor, Tyler Meier, Julie Johnson, Christine Baines, Renee Angle, as well as Susan Briante, Farid Matuk, Sam Ace, T. C. Tolbert, Sunny, and Rosie.

My NYU graduate students, especially the graduate students in my fall 2015 "Legacy of the Confessional Impulse" craft class. Your poems, questions, challenges, book suggestions, and struggles were vitally influential to these lectures.

MacDowell and everyone on the staff and all the other visiting artists for the twenty-eight bitterly glorious days in January of 2018 during which time these lectures became a book.

Also: the poet-moms listserv, Sally Ball, Catherine Barnett, Colin Beckett, Jeremy Bendik-Keymer, Julie Carr, James Ciano, Chris Doire, Thomas Dooley, Miranda Field, Devereux Fortuna, Nicholas Fuenzalida, Hafizah Geter, Joshua Goren, Moses Zucker Goren, Arielle Greenberg, Yona Harvey, Cathy Park Hong, Joy Katz, Becca Klaver, Wayne Koestenbaum, Christine Larusso, Katy Lederer, Jen Levitt, Deirdre Lord, Erin Murray Marra, Erika Meitner, Michael Miller, David Mindich, Jeremy Mindich, Lisa Moore, David Naimon, Alice Notley, Sharon Olds, Lisa Olstein, Joan Platt, D. A. Powell, Mike Sakasegawa,

Jason Schneiderman, Daniel Shiffman, Laurel Snyder, Mark Stabile, Soren Stockman, Camille Rankine, Claudia Rankine, David Trinidad, Doreen Wang, Benjamin Zucker.

Heidi Broadhead (and everyone at Wave), Isaac Ginsberg Miller, and Toby Mirroff—thank you more than I can say or write. There would be no book without you.